Mastering the Law of Attraction for Money

17 Secret Manifestation Techniques to Quickly Attract Wealth, Success, and Abundance

Layla Moon

Layla Moon

Layla Moon

Table of Contents

4 FREE Gifts

To help you along your spiritual journey, I've created 4 FREE bonus eBooks.

You can get instant access by signing up to my email newsletter below.

On top of the 4 free books, you will also receive weekly tips along with free book giveaways, discounts, and so much more.

All of these bonuses are 100% free with no strings attached. You don't need to provide any personal information except your email address.

To get your bonus, go to:

https://dreamlifepress.com/four-free-gifts

Or scan the QR code below

SCAN ME

Spirit Guides for Beginners: How to Hear the Universe's Call and Communicate with Your Spirit Guide and Guardian Angels

Guided by Moon herself, inspired by her own experiences and knowledge that has been passed down by hundreds of generations for thousands of years, you'll discover everything you need to know to;

- Understanding what the call of the universe is
- How to hear and comprehend it
- Knowing who and what your spirit guides and guardian angels are
- Learning how to connect, start a conversation, and listen to your guides
- How to manifest your dreams with the help of the cosmic source
- Learning how to start living the life you want to live
- And so much more…

Law of Attraction: Manifest Your Desire

Learn how to tap into the infinite power of the universe and manifest everything you want in life.

Includes:

- Law of Attraction: Manifest Your Desire ebook
- Law of Attraction Workbook
- Cheat sheets and checklists so make sure you're on the right path

Hoodoo Book of Spells for Beginners: Easy and effective Rootwork, Conjuring, and Protection Spells for Healing and Prosperity

Harness the power of one of the greatest magics. Hoodoo is a powerful force ideal for holding negativity at bay, promoting positivity in all areas in your life, offering protection to the things you love, and ultimately taking control of your destiny.

Inside, you will discover:
- How to get started with Hoodoo in your day-to-day life
- How to use conjuration spells to manifest the life you want to live
- How casting protection spells can help you withstand the toughest of times
- Break cycles of bad luck and promote good fortune throughout your life
- Hoodoo to encourage prosperity and financial stability
- How to heal using Hoodoo magic, both short-term and long-term traumas and troubles
- Remove curses and banish pain, suffering, and negativity from your life
- And so much more…

Book of Shadows

A printable PDF to support you in your spiritual transformation.

Within the pages, you will find:

- Potion and tinctures tracking sheet
- Essential oils log pages
- Herbs log pages
- Magical rituals and spiritual body goals checklist
- Tarot reading spread sheets
- Weekly moon and planetary cycle tracker
- And so much more

Get all the resources for FREE by visiting the link below

https://dreamlifepress.com/four-free-gifts

Introduction

Take a moment to yourself and settle in. As you read this opening line, chances are you've sat somewhere relaxing, perhaps on a sofa or in bed, and you're ready to dive in. But you're not clutching your Kindle or flicking through pages to read the next *Harry Potter* or *Me Before You*.

You're here because you want your life to change and you're ready to start making changes.

The reason you've picked up this book, and perhaps many others like it in the past, is because there's something about yourself or your life that you're not content with. I want you to use this moment to figure out what it is.

Maybe you already know. You don't have enough money, you're in debt, or you're just not earning enough to live the life you want. Perhaps your relationship with those you love has fallen on hard times and you're trying to figure out how to create more peaceful, more fulfilling, and more meaningful relationships. Your issues could be anything, from your health and wellbeing to your mindset, family, or career. Chances are... it's a tangle of multiple things.

This book contains the answers. This book contains the guidance to help you resolve these issues. Throughout the following chapters, you'll learn the strategies and techniques, all actionable, to manifest the life you want to live. The reality you'll be waking up to everyday. The reality you've been waking up to every single day of your life so far.

All by hyper-focusing on one primary aspect of your life.

Your success.

On this journey, we'll explore the ins and outs of the 17 techniques which will be broken down throughout the book into three core elements; Wealth. Success. Abundance.

If you can manifest and attract these three things into your life, you'll be able to unlock brand-new opportunities to live the life you want. We cannot change the fact that the world relies on money; you need to pay bills, have a house, or a job. This is the collective manifested reality of the entire human race that dates back thousands of years.

But that's not what we're focusing on today. Today, we're focusing on you, and your reality.

You are more than capable of living the life you want. You are allowed to have enough money to live in the house you want, to support your family the way you want, to have a car, to afford to travel, and to have the things you desire. You are allowed to have time to work on your business ideas, your passion projects, or to get to a point in your career where you feel accomplished.

All these things are within your grasp, just a few steps from where you are, and it's these steps we're going to explore throughout this book. However, these steps are founded on one core law that governs everything in our universe and reality, down to an atomic level.

The Law of Attraction

The Law of Attraction is one of the most powerful laws in the universe. Simply stated, the law maintains that 'Like Attracts Like.' But when applied to your own life, it's a power that can change your life in a sustainable and meaningful way.

The law states that what we focus on expands and comes back to us. Essentially, your life and reality are a reflection of what is going on in your mind, what your thoughts are and, therefore, what kind of energy and perspective you're putting out into the world.

On the surface, this is a very easy concept to grasp and apply in your life. If you spend time around toxic, negative people, then you will channel that same energy. There's a popular psychological saying that states, 'you're the average of the five people you surround yourself with the most,' because you take on their traits and the same energy bounces off.

Regardless of what you believe, if you're around people who don't share the same values as you, you might get along civilly, but you probably won't spend all your time together. For example, when I was growing up, I was friends with a boy called David, but as we grew older, into our late teens, we drifted apart. We were still friends and sometimes hung out, but he'd developed a drug habit.

While taking drugs frequently is not a value of mine, it was a value of his (for a number of reasons), and he surrounded himself with people who shared the same ideas. Of course, taking drugs frequently is not a good idea and it's going to lead down a dangerous and toxic path, which is what happened. He ended up in a rough patch where he was stealing money from his family, lying to those he loved and who loved him, and eventually he was admitted to hospital after he overdosed.

It's a sad story, and thankfully over the years he has taken steps to head down a different path, but it's clear how he got himself in that position in the first place. If you're in a negative space and you're putting negative energy out into the world, this is what you'll get back. Despite a desperate situation, he always had a choice at every stage of his journey of how he could move forward, something he now admits, but this is something I'm sure we can all relate to.

Let's say you spent eight hours a day watching a news program that focused on the problems of the COVID-19 pandemic, the Ukraine war, corrupt police officers, and engaged in plenty of discussions describing how horrible people are and how much of a bad condition the world is currently in. Over time, you're going to have a very miserable life believing that everything is negative, the world is in an awful state and the world we live in is a horrible place. Perhaps you've felt it after consuming too much news or social media content.

Yes, these are all important topics that we should be aware of, but deep-diving into them is going to drastically affect your mentality. You may have experienced this at work when people are gossiping about other coworkers. You end up being in a surreal anxious trap where you don't trust anyone around you out of fear of them talking about you, and so you gossip more, projecting your own insecurities. It's a toxic cycle that ultimately ends up affecting every other aspect of your life.

You wake up hating the idea of going to work, and you're miserable during the working week. Because you're unhappy, you project this onto your partner and you start having arguments. You seek out ways to feel better and start indulging in material objects and spending money, thus your financial situation gets tight.

Meanwhile, all the goals and dreams you wanted to fulfill throughout your life have taken a backseat and now you're resenting yourself because you're not living the life you want to live, and this only makes you hate your job and life circumstances more and the cycle spins out of control. Before you know it, you're not performing well at work and your job is at risk. Your partner doesn't want to be with you anymore. Your coping mechanisms are costing you your money and your health.

Of course, these are just examples, but they show the very

simple yet life-changing power of the energy you put out into the universe. However, these examples show that your actions and decisions are happening mindlessly. You're not conscious. You're just reacting to how you feel without taking the time to actually think about what you're doing.

David fueled his drug addiction because of his physical and mental cravings. He wasn't thinking about what would come next. We know that stealing from the people we love and care about is wrong, yet it's still something people do. You know it's wrong to shout and hurl abuse at your partner, but it still happens sometimes. And guess what, when you send that negative energy out, your partner won't like you much, and you get the negative energy back.

Embracing the Law of Attraction is about taking control.

When you start applying this law to certain aspects of your life, like your wealth and success, you can really start manifesting the kind of reality you want to enjoy. At the end of the day, if you can address these specific areas, they will have a huge knock-on effect on the rest of your life, including your happiness, wellbeing, relationships, and overall fulfillment with love.

The Law of Attraction is not just some New Age nonsense. It is a real, proven law, referenced by some of the top minds in human history, and by some of the most successful and wealthiest people in the world. The concepts that contribute to the Law of Attraction have been demonstrated by scientists and researchers all over the world, and throughout the decades.

Of course, the Law of Attraction is not just about manifesting money. You can use it to manifest any desire you have, but financial abundance will be our primary focus in this book. In order to manifest money using the Law of Attraction, you need to know how to apply its principles in a way that is specific to money. You need to figure out and understand how you think; defining what kind of energy you're putting out, therefore defining what energy you're getting back.

But let's not get ahead of ourselves. We'll take it step-by-step and break it down as we go. In this book, I will teach you 17 secret techniques that will help you quickly attract wealth, success, and abundance.

But first, let me share how this journey has been for me.

My Own Journey

A few years ago, I was in a rut. Financially, I've never been in a worse position.

After years in a corporate job that literally made me unwell, I built up my confidence and eventually took the leap of faith and started my own business. I gave it everything. All my confidence and savings. I left my abusive relationship to truly focus on me and to follow my dreams of being independent. I told everyone and was so excited. Terrified, but excited to start this new chapter.

And it failed.

Despite investing everything I had to try and make it work, it just wasn't meant to be. Maybe the market was wrong (there was an economic crash around the same time that I didn't pay nearly enough attention to), or maybe I just took the wrong approach. I didn't take the right steps at the right time, or didn't know what I needed to do.

Of course, while I was disappointed and felt like a complete failure, I had a life to rebuild. Life wasn't going to stop, so after a brief grieving period where I had to move into a friend's apartment because I couldn't afford rent, I took stock of where I was.

I had a lot of debt and no money to pay it off. I was working two jobs, but it wasn't enough to cover the costs, nor was it enough to get me back on my feet. I was stressed out and miserable.

I'd sold everything I'd owned including my car, moved out of my apartment, and crashed on friends' sofas. I was ashamed of my situation. I was borrowing money from friends to pay off other friends and family, and I was stuck in this loop of earning and spending everything on debt.

Despite the bleakness of my situation, I was plagued by the need to escape this reality, and I was trying everything and anything I could to make a difference. My mental health and self-esteem were at an all time low. I tried different saving strategies, switched jobs several times, tried money management techniques, bullet journaling, apps, and a friend organized a free consultation with her financial advisor friend. However, nothing seemed to click.

Then, one day, I was introduced to the Law of Attraction. I met up with a friend who was reading *The Secret* and it sparked something inside me. This wasn't something I was new to. My grandmother on my mother's side used the Law of Attraction every single day, and growing up I would regularly see her meditating, journaling, or making vision boards, but I rarely paid any attention to it.

The idea had now come back into my life via my friend and the online articles and podcasts I dove into, and I continued to feel the shift. I went deeper. I read more books, watched more videos, and listened to more podcasts. I learned about the principles of vibration, both spiritually and scientifically, and piece by piece, as my knowledge and understanding of the law grew and expanded, I began to meaningfully apply the teachings to my own life.

While I certainly had a ton to sort out in my life, my main focus to begin with was my financial situation. There was no doubt this was the area of my life that was causing the most stress, and I knew that once I sorted it out, I could then focus on everything else.

For example, I could join a gym for my physical health, and see a therapist for my mental health. I could get an apartment to build back up my independence and a car to get access to the careers I wanted. And so, I began to focus on my desires for money and wealth. I visualized myself in a situation where I had plenty of money. I focused on the feeling of having enough money, and I repeated affirmations like 'I am abundant,' 'I am prosperous,' and 'I am wealth,' every single day.

I told myself that money comes to me easily and effortlessly and that I always have more than enough money, among other techniques that I experimented with and adjusted along the way. These techniques took some trial and error, but eventually, and in some cases even as quickly as a couple of days, I felt a shift in my being and perspective. My life began to truly change.

Over the course of a year, I paid off all my debts, but I didn't stop there. I was also able to build up my savings and get a job that I was happy in and paid me my worth, which in turn allowed me to get an apartment, a car, and the things I had desired at the beginning.

I'm not saying it was easy. It was a journey, for sure. There were ups, downs, and hard times. There were times on the climb when I slipped, but the techniques helped me find my footing and keep going relatively easily.

Fast forward several years, the Law of Attraction is something that I apply to my life daily, manifesting my reality in whatever ways I want. Over the years, I discovered my passion for writing and being creative, a career that I then manifested using these same techniques. The same applies to my relationships; professionally, personally, and romantically.

My beliefs regarding material objects and the way I make conscious decisions have all been influenced by the Law of Attraction.

These are the techniques and experiences I'm going to share with you, and they can work for you too. So, let's get started, first taking a detailed look into what the Law of Attraction actually is and how it works.

CHAPTER ONE

Getting Started

Live as if you were to die tomorrow; learn as if you were to live forever.

- Mahatma Gandhi

The Law of Attraction is known as different things to different people. To some, it is called the Law of Vibration. To others, it is called the Law of Focus. But they are all talking about the same thing. We'll stick with the Law of Attraction since this is the most popular term.

To use the Law of Attraction in your own life, you need to start by understanding how it works. To teach is to show what is possible. To learn is to make it possible for yourself, so take on board what I'm saying, but I highly recommend exploring each concept so you maximize the chances of it making sense to you. But don't worry, I'll guide you along the way.

Let's start with the five basic principles of the Law of Attraction, which include:

1. Thoughts and emotions create vibrations that attract similar vibrations. Like attracts Like.

2. What we focus on expands.

3. We attract what we are vibrating at the frequency of.

4. Our thoughts and emotions create our reality.

5. You can use the Law of Attraction to manifest any type of desire you have.

Taking these into account, the Law of Attraction isn't some kind of magic or cosmic concept, but is grounded in science, founded on the principle of vibration, which has been proven by scientists and researchers all over the world, which is also why the two terms are commonly used interchangeably.

However, more correctly, the Law of Attraction comes second, and the Law of Vibration is the first universal law.

Introducing the Law of Vibration

In the words of Bob Proctor, 'we live in an ocean of motion.' Everybody, including this book, talks about the Law of Attraction and how you can use it to manifest the life you've always wanted, but in truth, LoA is the all-encompassing term for manifestation and attracting. How it works is using the Law of Vibration.

Dr. Lipton, a cell biologist who has dedicated his life to understanding the principles of how cells work, is one of the most famous scientists who has researched the principle of vibration. He has found that the behavior of cells is controlled by their environment, which includes the thoughts and emotions of the person who is observing them.

This groundbreaking discovery has helped support the theory that the Law of Attraction is based on science. When we think positive thoughts and feel positive emotions, we are putting ourselves into a vibration that is in harmony with our desires. And, when we maintain this positive vibration, we are more likely to attract what we want into our lives.

Everything in the universe, from every galaxy and planet to every atom, is constantly in motion. This motion is vibration, and everything vibrates at a specific frequency. This can be observed in sound waves. A low bass is a low-frequency sound wave, and if you watch it played from an exposed speaker, you'll see the speaker cones vibrating.

The Law of Vibration applies to everything.

Imagine a room in a community center. You could host any kind of event in this room and while the room remains the same, the vibration can be different. For example, if you hosted a surprise birthday party, the room will feel electric from the moment you walk in, immediately lifting your spirits and making you feel alive.

On the other hand, if you walk into the same room and there is a funeral service going on, the vibrations are low and solemn. You don't even need to be a part of the event to feel the energy. This is, quite literally, where the traditionally hippy term 'vibe' comes from. You can feel the 'vibe,' or the vibrations of a situation, wherever you go.

Let's say you enter a party room and you feel the electric vibe, your vibration then syncs with the vibration of the room and you'll be able to dance, laugh, and have a good time with people. You're manifesting happiness and positivity.

If you're a salesperson, your job is to sit down with prospective clients and get to them. Using your skills, you'll tune in to the frequency, or 'the vibe,' of the other person through asking questions and reading their body language. Using this information, you'll try to match their frequency, tuning in to their wants and needs, then being able to sell your product or service in the best possible way.

This is the same reason you can feel uncomfortable around some people. If you're in a really positive mood (a high vibration), but you're surrounded by negative people who are in a bad mood, you'll feel out of place, isolated, and feel that something isn't right. This is because the frequency of your vibrations and everyone else's doesn't align, and you feel the difference. If you stay around these negative vibrations for too long, and they're the main vibrations in the room, then slowly (or sometimes very quickly), your vibrations will align with theirs, and you'll feel the same, thus crashing your mood.

Whatever the situation, it's important to remember that these vibrations can't be touched or seen. You can feel or sense them, and you can certainly react to them.

As you can see, it's a simple concept, but the consequences can be far-reaching. To tie this in with the Law of Attraction, the real power in these concepts is that you can control the vibrations of your life. Consciously and mindfully, you can manifest the life you want to live.

Using the Law of Attraction

Using the Law of Vibration, you can master the art of the Law of Attraction by literally controlling the frequencies in which you and the universe around you vibrates. This is what it means to manifest your dreams and desires. This is what it means to manifest your reality.

The Law of Attraction is about embodying the right vibration to manifest your desires. Don't be fooled. This isn't a book about positive thinking or hoping for the best with all your willpower. Sure, positive thinking and believing in your actions and desires are a part of the process, but it's not all there is. It's about intentionally managing and controlling your thoughts and actions to manifest the reality you want, to fulfill your desires, and to live the life you want.

This is about changing everything. The shocking truth is, the Law of Attraction is working all the time. Right now, your entire being, thoughts, emotions, and actions are putting a vibrational frequency out into the universe and that energy is coming back to you.

This change will happen to you, regardless of whether you're in control of it or not. The Law of Attraction will affect your life, whether you know or believe it exists, or not. Think about your life ten years ago, and where you are now.

Using the Law of Attraction, you can actually do several things. I've touched on manifesting your reality. If you want to experience the same joy you would feel walking into a positive situation, you need to raise your vibration to that frequency. If you want a fulfilling relationship, you need to raise your vibration to the experience of a fulfilling relationship.

If you want to attract wealth and success in everything you do, you need to raise your vibration to feeling wealthy and successful. There are many ways to do this, all of which we'll explore throughout the book.

So, if you focus on something with strong emotional energy, you will begin to vibrate at the same frequency as that thing.

A Note Before We Start

While these Law of Attraction techniques can be adapted and applied to all kinds of aspects of your life, this book is going to focus on three main aspects of your life; wealth, success, and abundance. But to start manifesting and working with them, we need to dive into what they are and how they are defined.

What is Wealth?

Wealth is one of the most interesting concepts in humanity. Sure, the most basic definition, perhaps the one that came to mind, is that it is the ability to generate an income that exceeds your expenses. The generic definition of being 'wealthy' is someone who has lots of money in their bank accounts and to whom money is not really an issue in their day-to-day life. It's not a stressful life factor as it would be with someone who's living from paycheck to paycheck.

However, in reality, wealth is far more diverse than just this. Whereas you can be wealthy with money, you can also be wealthy with the freedom that money gives you. When you're not stressing about how you're going to pay your bills, you can pour that attention into other things that matter to you, like following your passion or helping your community.

Wealth is not just about money. You can be wealthy in your health, family, and relationships. You can be wealthy in love or in experiences. You can find a form of wealth in writing or being creative. What you can be wealthy in depends on you as an individual and what matters to you. Therefore, the definition of wealth can vary from person to person.

I'm not saying that being financially wealthy is a bad thing. Again, being financially stable brings freedom. If you want to look after your family, you need money. If you want to travel or start a business, you need money. But being wealthy is not just about money, so it's important to make sure you're not put off by this idea. Instead, start to redefine what wealth means to you.

Yes, maybe you don't believe that living in the capitalist world we find ourselves in is a good thing. You may think the rich are the bane of it, and you may believe that consumerism, fast fashion, sweatshops in eastern countries, and the throw-away culture that has permeated the world is a negative thing, but these aren't all tied to the idea of being 'wealthy.' This is more about people's values, their views, and quest for material possessions, short-term, rapid validation, and desire for status in any form. It's not necessarily money that's the problem. It's the views and perspectives of the people who have it.

If you want to do good, whether that's saving animals, providing healthcare aid to families living in war-torn countries, or you want to help treat cancer, you need money to make it happen.

There's a famous video of wildlife conservationist and television host Steve Irwin talking about this.

"What good is a fast car, a flashy house, and a gold plated dunny to me? Absolutely no good at all. I've been put on this planet to protect wildlife and wilderness areas. Which in essence is going to help humanity. I want to have the purest oceans. I want to stop the ozone layer. I want to save the world. And you know money? Money's great. I can't get enough money. And you know what I'm going to do with it? I'm going to buy wilderness areas with it. Every single cent I get goes straight into conservation, and what, I don't give a rip who's money it is mate. I'll use it and I'll spend it on buying land."

Steve Irwin is an icon for a reason. He was wealthy in his relationships and in his love for animals. He was living his dream and fulfilling his purpose in the world, making him a very wealthy man in many aspects.

Having money or generic financial wealth doesn't make you rich. You don't need to have millions in the bank or a ton of investments to be happy. Instead, you should have money in a way that works for you. Make money mean something to you in a way that fulfills your goals and your life's purpose; not something to strive for in itself. Sure, if you want millions of dollars out of greed for material objects, a large house, and a nice car, by all means go for it if it makes you happy. However, for the vast majority of people, this doesn't really work out, and they end up feeling more unfulfilled than ever before.

Think of money as a way of taking opportunities that come your way. For most people, having enough money to live comfortably, to provide for their families, to pay for things without having to take out credit, and not worry when the next paycheck is coming in is enough.

However, it can mean whatever you want it to mean. Just try to have a clear idea of what this is, a process we'll explore later in more detail.

What is Success?

Just like wealth, ask yourself what success means to you. Sure, when you first think about it, you might think of things like having a well-paying job or owning your own business, being respected or having authority within your community, in the public eye, or within your social circles. However, success can be way more than that.

It could be as simple as being happy and fulfilled in what you do each day or providing value to the people around you. It could be raising a healthy and happy family. It could be making a contribution to society that improves the quality of life for others.

Success doesn't have to mean anything specific, but it's important to have an idea of what it means to you. When you do, you can start to put in place the things that will get you there.

What is Abundance?

The third and final area we're going to focus on is abundance. Abundance is usually defined as having more than enough. However, when it comes to the Law of Attraction, abundance is about having enough of what you need or want, not only in relation to yourself, but to the world as well.

Just because there are tens of thousands of other best-selling authors, music artists, or people who own successful pressure washing businesses, it doesn't mean that you can't be successful or thrive in these areas.

This can feel like an abstract concept, but it's a mindset you can work towards. The more you focus on abundance and the good things in your life, the more you'll see them come your way.

According to the Law of Attraction, there is more than enough of everything to go around, especially to those who want it. When you think about it that way, it becomes even more special. If there are so many other people who have set out into the world to achieve something and they've succeeded, this shows that it's possible, and there's no reason why you can't do it too.

You can have whatever you want in life. Just because someone else has or had it doesn't mean you can't get it.

When it comes to attracting money, abundance, and success into your life, it's important to have a clear idea of what these things mean to you. Just as each person is unique, so too are the definitions of these words for each individual.

And with that, we're ready to take the first steps into making the Law of Attraction work for you. Take a deep breath, and let's get into it.

Now that we've covered the basics and have built a theoretical understanding of what we'll explore throughout the book, I want you to take a moment to yourself. This is where we'll discuss the first technique that will help you discover the secrets behind manifestation.

Technique #1 - Remind Yourself You're Alive

This technique is a short and simple one designed to get you started on your journey into using the Law of Attraction to manifest wealth and success. It's designed to help you shift your mind into the present moment, as well as help you start to not only notice your vibrational frequency, but also change it to a frequency you want.

Start by taking a nice, deep breath through the nose. Hold for a few seconds, and exhale nice and slowly through your mouth. The proper timing for this is breathing in for four seconds, holding for five seconds, and then exhaling for six seconds. However, you can go with what works for you, as long as the durations of each breath are relatively long. The longer your timings, the better. Repeat three times.

Do you feel that peaceful energy? Take a moment to feel the sensation of your body sitting on your chair. That feeling of contact. The feeling of your weight pushing down, gravity weighing on you. This is a great time to perform a guided meditation using an app or YouTube video, but the three breaths should be enough.

Once you're feeling peaceful and calm, and your mind relatively still, take this moment of solitude to reflect on how much has changed in your life over the last few years. Say you're 30. Statistically speaking, you have decades of time left.

All those years. So much time. Realize how many days and months and years you have to live over and over again. How many opportunities and chances to grow you'll have during this time. Even if you have less time, use this as inspiration to use your time even more wisely.

The point is, just like the last however many years you've been alive, things are going to happen to you and you are going to do things and regardless of how long your life is, you are going to live. You are living your life right now.

So why not make it a life you're actually excited to wake up to? Why not live a life you're actually happy, peaceful, and content with? Why not aim for something bigger, greater, and more satisfying than where you are now?

Manifesting your desired reality is a process, and there will be ups and downs as you learn, but ultimately, you want to become the best version of yourself, whatever that means to you. This is a technique you'll want to practice often, and yes, it really is that simple.

No matter where you find yourself in life, no matter what you're doing, or who you're with, take a few seconds to take these three deep breaths, recenter yourself, and realize that you're living your life right here, right now. Notice how the colors around you become even more vibrant and beautiful with this realization. Notice how grateful you feel for having the opportunity to not only live a life, but to actually live the life you want. You can make it happen.

Practice daily - several times a day if you really want to maximize the effect.

This is what the Law of Attraction is all about.

CHAPTER 2

Abundant Mind vs Poor Mind

"Acknowledging the good that you already have in your life is the foundation for all abundance."

– Eckhart Tolle

A quote worth thinking about.

When it comes to living your life, your mindset is everything. By mindset, I'm referring to the set of beliefs you hold that come together to shape your perspective. Your mindset is basically the series of thoughts you have when it comes to understanding and making your way through the world. Your mindset influences everything, from what you think to how you feel, and basically defines how you make decisions in any given situation.

When it comes to the Law of Attraction, your mindset sets your vibrational frequency based on the thoughts you think and the decisions you make. While there are a near-infinite number of ways to categorize your mindset, we're going to focus on two; the abundant mindset and the poor mindset.

Financially, how well off you are or aren't doesn't play into this. You can be a wealthy person with a poor mindset, just as you can be financially poor but have a rich mindset. But remember, 'rich' doesn't just refer to having money. It also means having time to do the things you want, abundance, success in terms of positioning and manifesting your desires, and being content, peaceful, and happy.

I could easily cut this chapter short by saying that if you want more money, more time, better health, or to be rich in any way, you'll need to work on your mindset. Even a small and simple shift in your mindset can make a huge difference to your wealth, and your entire life.

But what's the difference between the two?

What is a Poor Mindset?

A poor mindset is one that is closed off to wealth, money, and success. To have a poor mindset is to have a negative attitude towards the thing you want. For example, a poor mindset believes that money is the root of all evil. You may associate money with pain, struggle, and deprivation. As a result, a poor mindset person does everything they can to avoid money.

This could be through hoarding, excessive spending, or even just not earning enough money. Even if you feel like you want money to live your dreams, you'll unconsciously stand in your own way and hold yourself back from having money if you have a poor mindset.

In my own life, especially during my early twenties, I was chronically in debt and had thrown so much money at my failed business. Seeing myself in debt every time I opened my bank account and saw the figures in red, meeting up with a friend who I owed money to, or even having others offer to pay my lunch bill because they knew I was in a bad position only reaffirmed these beliefs I had.

Working three jobs while trying to get out of debt only to save for a while, make several large payments or repayments, and then find myself back at square one amplified this belief. Even though I knew that getting out of debt and seeking financial security was a long-term process, that didn't stop me from feeling incapable and stressed.

All these thoughts and feelings led me to believe that I was incapable of managing my money properly, prone to making poor investment decisions, and lacked what it takes to be rich. I had consequently developed a poor mindset.

When you have a poor mindset, you live in constant fear that you're never going to have enough. You hold yourself back and stand in your own way because you're convinced that your circumstances are never going to change and you'll be stuck where you are for the rest of your life. Like attracts like, and because you're thinking these things, this is the reality you'll manifest. The purpose of your journey and reading this book is to break through these obstacles and change how you think, therefore changing your life.

The state of your mindset determines how you manage everything in your life, including the quality of your relationships, finances, energy levels, health, and resources like time. Poor minded people do this poorly.

People with a poor mindset are focused on short-term gains.

If they see an abundance or overflow of resources, to them it's an opportunity to consume. For example, if they receive a Christmas bonus at work, they spend it all on a vacation, a new car, or something that provides short-term satisfaction. Of course, chasing short-term satisfaction is not a great technique for achieving long-term fulfillment.

Those with a poor mindset are unwilling to invest or look to the future because they want things now. Of course, short-term pleasures don't bring long-term happiness. The happiness you receive from getting a new car is limited and fleeting, but a poor-minded person knows no better.

Therefore, they find themselves trapped in a loop of seeking ways to earn money, get healthy, or increase energy levels, only to expend these resources rapidly once they hit a certain point, forcing them to fall back to the starting point, beginning the cycle once again. A poor-minded person is constantly chasing things.

In any given situation, a poor mindset will look for immediate gain. They'll ask what is in the situation for them and won't see the value in doing something if there's no clear benefit. For example, they might not see the purpose of attending a client meeting if there's no guarantee of getting work out of it.

Now, what about the other side?

What is a Rich Mindset?

Also known as 'abundant thinking,' a rich mindset is the opposite way of thinking about life. When you have a rich mindset, your mind values what you have, and believes there is more coming in the future. This can apply to money, but it's so much more than that.

A rich mindset is open and receptive to everything. They know that opportunities, money, time, and success are all possible now and in the future. They acknowledge, are grateful for, and accept what they have now and look to see what is coming in the future. This, in turn, brings happiness, opportunities, freedom, and abundance. People with a rich mindset don't associate money with joy, pleasure, and fulfillment, as a poor-minded person would, but rather as a tool that unlocks the doors to these things. Remember the Steve Irwin quote in the last chapter? He didn't care how he got money, where, or whom it came from. He was financially well off, not because he strived to be rich, but because he was accumulating money to help him fulfill his goals and his purpose on this planet.

However, it's important to note that values play a part in this because values vibrate at a certain frequency, like everything else in the universe. If Steve Irwin was to raise money to fight his cause through selling drugs that ended up hurting people, this wouldn't reflect his values of wanting to help make the world a better place. A rich minded person will, therefore, attract money in a sustainable way.

They will invest their resources in systems that will generate money over long periods of time rather than constantly trading their hours for dollars. However, unlike a poor minded person, the results of such investments aren't necessarily financial but could be in terms of opportunity, experiment, or future investments.

They're not trying to be a one-hit-wonder, go viral on a single video, or win the lottery. They would rather have businesses that provide and meet their personal values. They have a responsibility and set up their life in a way that allows them an abundance of time to do the things that matter to them, whether that's traveling, spending time with their family, or having experiences. They want to set themselves up in a way that they are consistently happy, content, secure, safe, and thriving.

Imagine a graph of happiness and fulfillment. A poor mind would be incredibly spiky, peaking rapidly then dropping low and slowly going up again, peaking, then dropping low once more, and simply repeating this cycle.

Alternatively, a rich mind's graph would show a consistently slow and steady rise without many extreme events. When you apply this kind of concept to how you're living your life, you should be able to see the difference.

What Determines Your Mindset?

What determines whether you have a poor or abundant mind? We've focused on the broad aspects of abundant and poor mindsets and how that can apply to every aspect of your life, but this book is about finances, so what determines an abundant or poor mindset in this area of your life?

There are many factors and potentially a lot of variables, but one of the primary things that determine mindset is your environment and what you expose yourself to. If all you ever watch on TV or read in books is mired with negativity, it will be very hard for you to have a positive mindset.

This is particularly relevant in today's world because you can constantly compare yourself with other people. Whether you're watching celebrities on TV or following them on Instagram, you're constantly bombarded with the image that people are better off than you and have more than you do. This makes you crave the kind of life they have, making you ungrateful for yours.

Over time, this creates a poor mindset where you're more inclined to make impulsive purchases, like buying the latest iPhone or a new car, because you want the short-term rush of having nice things. Because you crave the rush, you're constantly spending money and living in the paycheck to paycheck rut.

Then, when you find inspiration and have an idea for a business or you want to invest in one, you won't have the capital to invest and your journey into bringing your dream to life is going to be so much more difficult. Say you've been dating someone for a while and you're ready to marry, start a family, and move into together, and now you need a deposit for a mortgage, but you don't have it because of your lifestyle choices.

This experience could have you regretting your past decisions, but it also reaffirms your belief that you're bad at handling money. Then you compare yourself to the friends and peers who are homeowners and feel even worse, sinking deeper into your poor mindset.

On the other hand, if you plan to save for a new car but you're faced with an unexpected bill and cover it easily with minimal disruption to the rest of your life, this is proof that you're managing your money well, reaffirming your abundant mindset.

Everything you are, past and present experiences, and even the views of your parents and the people you've grown up with, all play into what you believe about the world and how you see yourself. If your parents constantly berated you and told you that you were awful at managing your finances and you need to be better, this is what you'll tell yourself and what you'll always believe - and it will remain your reality until you're able to break these thought patterns and switch up your mindset.

Technique #2: Develop a Rich Mindset

To develop a rich mindset, you need to figure out what your current beliefs are. Once you understand them and where they come from (basically defining why you think the way you do), you can start changing your thoughts. You can adjust your perspective into one that serves you. This will change your vibrational frequency, the energy you're sending out into the universe, the energy you're receiving back, ultimately manifesting the reality you want.

This is a life-long process, but it's not a difficult process. At least it doesn't have to be.

This technique is nice and easy; it is actionable and will use the

Law of Attraction to help you increase your wealth as well as help you move towards a richer mindset.

Through this process, you're going to become a mindful spender. This means becoming mindful and conscious of how and when you're spending your money, what you're spending your money on, and basically breaking the spending habits borne of a poor mindset. From now on, you're going to be spending money with a rich mindset.

Recently, I really wanted to purchase an Apple Watch. My partner has one and I want one to help with my productivity tracking and health goals, such as running reminders, heart rate monitoring, water tracking and so on. In the past, when I had a poorer mindset, I would just instantly pay for it and get it shipped the next day. However, the amount of money spent would make me feel ashamed and stressed, especially when I ended up struggling to afford my bills and debt repayments.

However, with an abundance mindset, I know that I need to prioritize paying my bills and debts, and saving money, and that I will have money in the future and the opportunity to buy the watch if I still want one.

This was not an easy decision. I already had the Watch in the online cart and I was ready to check it out, but I didn't. Instead,

I recognized that the watch isn't something I need now as I have more responsible purchases that will attract money in the future. For now, I remain grateful for what I have.

And it was that simple. A poor mindset switched into an abundant one. I just saved myself $400 which I can spend on more appropriate, beneficial purchases, and a ton of potential stress. So, try this yourself, but start small.

With this in mind, for the next 30 days (seven days if you're completely new to this), I want you to not buy anything. Okay, that's obviously impossible because you need to live, but this technique is all about saving your money for what's essential, and understanding that if you want to buy more luxury items, you can because you have more money coming in the future that you can use to spend more sustainably. Just because you have the money now doesn't mean you need to spend it.

Basically, for the next 30 days, do not buy anything except essentials or something you absolutely need.

That's it. You're not saving or trying to find cheaper or more affordable ways of doing things. You're simply not buying anything that isn't essential. When you have an impulse to buy something, ask yourself whether it's important or if it can wait, and be conscious with your decisions, not frivolous.

How does this tie into the Law of Attraction? Well, every single time you want to make a purchase, you're consciously thinking about whether it's essential and making a decision.

It's this process of thinking intentionally that will put the energy out into the universe that you're now managing your money essentially, and only making purchases that matter. On top of this, you're saying that money is now a resource that you're only saving for essential things and that you're going to be investing in long-term resources that will sustainably bring value to your life.

Also, bear in mind that you are going to face challenges, but there are plenty of actionable tips and questions you can ask yourself to help you face them;

- Develop a spending budget. Add up how much you earn, how much you spend on essential purchases, and where the rest goes. Understand where every single dollar you earn is going.

- Do you have triggers that make you spend impulsively? Do you buy things when you're feeling stressed, sad, or as a coping mechanism?

- Do you believe that buying material goods will make you

happy or satisfy/fulfill you?

Technique #3: The Hard Cut

Once you start being more conscious with your current spending, you can start focusing on your finances by managing your money more sustainably and responsibly. Remember, building a solid foundation of spending habits is essential if you want to be wealthy and successful. It doesn't matter whether you have $100 in the bank or $100,000, if you can't look after your money, you're going to lose it.

Looking at my own accounts, I chose to create shopping lists (even if I listed a bar of chocolate every now and then because it was a treat that made me happy), canceled the Netflix and gym subscriptions I wasn't using, and stopped impulsively purchasing books.

This is called the hard cut, and it's essential. Go through your accounts for the last few months and see what you've spent money on. Cancel all subscriptions that you don't need or don't serve you, and add up how much money you've spent on coffees, expensive lunch dates, clothes, video games, and other non-essential expenses.

Yes, this can be hard to look at, but you have to face the reality of your situation to prove to the universe that you're willing to do whatever it takes to turn your life around. This is the energy you'll put out, and the energy you'll be getting back. If you don't want to look because you're afraid or ashamed of your spending habits, this is the energy you'll send out, and you'll remain stuck.

By using both techniques, I saved well over $400 in just 30 days. It wasn't much, but at the time, it meant everything.

Still applying this same logic today, I have money for a rainy day, savings, and can afford unexpected bills. I'm financially secure and with every interaction I have with money, I'm putting the same rich mindset vibrational frequencies out into the universe, ensuring that the same energy comes back to me.

CHAPTER 3

Unconscious Money Blocks Keeping You From Financial Freedom

"Stop standing in your own way. Stop making excuses. Stop talking about why you can't. Stop sabotaging yourself. Decide which direction you are going in and take action. One decision at a time, one moment at a time."

— Akiroq Brost

There's a reason you struggle to create a life you're happy to live. There's a reason you constantly try to make your life better but constantly feel like you fall back to square one time and time again. Ever thought about finally sorting out your financial situation only to be no better off after months of putting in work?

The reason the world of financial freedom always seems out of reach is because you have money blocks. In addition to figuring out where you are today and how you can make your financial situation better in a proactive and actionable way, you also need to spend time figuring out and overcoming the unconscious blocks and thought patterns.

The mental blocks you have when it comes to finances, whether you're conscious of their existence or not, are preventing you from having money. For example, if you think money is the root of all evil, then you're always going to be financially poor, because even though you may want money to live your life, your belief means you're always going to push it away.

In my own life, I always referred to myself as not having enough money, not having the skills to look after money responsibly, and not being worthy of money. I believed that I just didn't have what it takes to have money and to spend it wisely or maturely, thus this was the reality I manifested.

The best thing you can do right now is become aware of your own blocks. Once you're aware of them, you can begin figuring out where they came from, how you can let them go, and how you can replace them with thoughts and perspectives that will actually serve you in your ventures instead of holding you back and keeping you stuck in a rut.

When it comes to manifesting money, there are a few unconscious blocks that can keep you from achieving your goals, and we're going to explore them here. What's more, we're going to explore some powerful techniques for overcoming each one.

The Fear of Not Having Enough Money

One of the biggest blocks to manifesting money is the fear of not having enough. This fear can be caused by a variety of factors, including past experiences with money, negative beliefs about money, or lack of financial education.

When you affirm thoughts like 'I do not have enough money,' this is the reality you're manifesting. If you're afraid that you need to buy something now because you don't believe or you're not conscious of the fact you'll have money in the future (a fear of not having money in the future), then you won't have money in the future.

It's not so much the fear of not having enough money that is holding you in place, it's the language of your thoughts. You're telling yourself that you won't have money in the future, so you don't. You're afraid your financial situation won't be positive in the future, and so it won't be. These are the thoughts affirming your reality that ultimately hold you in place and prevent you from becoming wealthy. The following statements affirm the same thing;

- I don't have enough money

- I never have enough

- I won't have enough money to pay my rent

- I'm screwed if my car breaks down and I need to fix it

- I am not prepared for unexpected bills or payments

- I don't know how I'm going to afford a vacation this year

It's these thoughts and statements that then become your truth, creating the energy you're sending out to the universe, manifesting a reality that is aligned with these statements.

The Fear of Success

Another common block to manifesting money is the fear of success. This is a fear many of us hold, one that is amplified by societal pressure. The fear of success is a very real unconscious block, and can hold you back on any kind of scale, whether that's fear of judgment from the wider public or simply anxious about what your partner may think of you. This is a fear that people might see you succeed and will become jealous, treating you differently.

You may think that with fame comes 'haters,' and you're not comfortable dealing with the negative impact. You may think your family and friends will treat you differently if you were to 'make it,' in whatever way you define this. Whatever your belief, this creates a fear of success that ends up causing you to not even try to do what you want to do, so you end up staying where you are, increasingly resenting yourself for not taking steps to live a fulfilling life.

You can be successful in all aspects of life. Success means different things to different people, whether that's;

- Getting the career you want

- Having a family

- Asking someone out on a date

- Starting your own business

- Starting a YouTube channel

- Joining a new club

- Picking up a new instrument

- Participating in a competition

Fear is a natural part of the process, whatever it is you plan on doing with your life. It's your mind's way of trying to predict problems you'll encounter so you can prepare for them and overcome them. However, these problems can easily be discouraging since you're always thinking of the worst-case scenarios, whereas in reality anything can happen and you can never really prepare for what's going to happen.

If you're thinking about writing a book, it's easy to think about all the time you're going to spend on the book, where you're going to find that time in your life, how you're going to write and make it sounds interesting, how you're going to develop your characters, and how difficult it is to get it into the hands of readers.

Yes, these are problems you'll have to overcome and sort out, but you can't hyperfocus on them. Doing so will strike fear into your heart and put you off trying at all. Instead, these are just part of the journey, and you need to balance this thinking with feelings of success, such as selling millions of books, people loving your stories, and you feeling creatively fulfilled.

However, some fears may be a little more obscure. Maybe you want to start a YouTube channel or social media page on something you care about, but you fear that the page will grow and you won't have enough time to post quality content consistently, so you get scared of the imagined growth and don't launch the page.

Perhaps your fear is founded in more general thought patterns, such as being fearful of change, or not wanting to step out of your comfort zone to change your routine. Maybe there are seemingly unrelated events in your past, such as unsupportive parents and events that have caused you to doubt your self-confidence, which end up holding you back.

The Fear Of Not Being Good Enough

Being successful and being good enough could seem like

interchangeable phrases in some ways, but they are different things, and everyone's definitions of the words vary considerably.

Success is relative. Fame, for example, is an easy concept to explore: if you're starting out in a small band and you sell ten albums at one gig, this could be far more albums than you've ever sold in your life, and you could be extremely happy with the progress you're making. On the other hand, if you're Lady Gaga, selling ten albums is extremely catastrophic for your career.

However, both the small band and Lady Gaga can experience the same fear of not being good enough. Lady Gaga might work on an album and even though it's very successful in terms of sales and fan reception, she can still feel like she's not good enough to release the music.

It's this fear of not being good enough that holds so many people back from doing the things they love, and it could be holding you back too. It's this fear that can stop you from taking certain actions and making certain decisions, such as;

- Starting a new passion project

- Asking for a raise

- Starting a business

- Accepting a position as a Best Man at a friend's wedding

- Joining a new gym or fitness class

- Not asking for a promotion

Having a Negative Mindset Towards Money

Another unconscious block you may have towards money may be related to your beliefs about other aspects of the world.

For example, if you have a negative mindset towards money, it will be far more difficult to manifest more of it, if any of it at all. This is because your thoughts and emotions can block the flow of money. There are a number of thought patterns that can contribute to this, such as;

- I believe rich people are evil and selfish

- Money causes so many problems in this world

- Having loads of wealth is greedy and selfish

- Having money means you will become greedy for materialistic things

- Having money means you're always at risk of losing all of

it

It's easy to develop a negative attitude and mindset towards money and finances if you've had bad experiences. What's more, all the content, entertainment, and media we consume helps push these ideas. For example, you might look at someone like Jeff Bezos, one of the richest men in the world, and think he's an awful person.

Money is a tool. Success is a journey. Wealth is a goal. It's time to break the molded beliefs that these things are inherently good or evil. They are not. They are neutral. They can, however, be used for good or evil, for manifesting positive or negative realities, depending on the person wielding them.

By identifying these beliefs in your life, you can begin to overcome them, and you'll be far more open to attracting wealth, success, and abundance in your life. After all, even if you want to raise money for charity for a cause that matters to you, or you want to be able to afford a house for your family to live safely in, no matter how badly you want it, if you have unconscious thoughts that money is bad, you'll unconsciously push it away, no matter how hard you try to attract it.

These beliefs could have been formed when you were growing up, from your friend groups and their beliefs, from your parents, from the media you consume, your immediate or nationwide communities and their beliefs, or your personal experiences.

If you've ever been in debt, this could have held you back in so many areas of your life, therefore it's easy to believe that money is a bad thing. After all, money has been the root of so many problems and stresses in your life for so many years. Over time, this builds up into a belief that money is a bad thing, so you convince yourself that you don't want more of it. The less you're thinking about money, the less likely you are to go back to where you were, but of course, this just isn't the case.

You're just putting out the vibrations of the reality you want to unconsciously manifest, which means pushing money away, rather than being a magnet for it.

With all these considerations in mind, having wealth, success, and abundance doesn't mean that you need to have millions in the bank. You need to define what these things mean to you. If having a secure job that pays $75,000 a year and helps you afford everything you want, allowing you to live securely without having the stresses of money weigh down on you is enough, then so be it. It's what matters to you.

However, if you want to get to that point, you're going to need to overcome the unconscious obstacles that are standing in your way.

Technique #4: Find What You Fear

Let's dive into our second secret to using the Law of Attraction, and that's going through the process of figuring out what your fears are. You have to go through this process because you need to know where you are now and what kind of thinking patterns you have so you can focus on changing them into thoughts that serve you.

It's acceptable to experience fear, but when it gets to the point where it's holding you back from the things you want to do and the life you want, it's time to address it and do something about it. So, what can you do?

Start by taking a piece of paper, a journal, or a text document and write down every single fear you have. Don't think too much about it, and if something comes up that you don't really think applies to you, write it down anyway.

Setting a five- or ten-minute timer can help you stay focused on continuously writing whatever comes to mind. There are no right or wrong answers; you're just allowing your unconscious mind to flow and put whatever onto the page. There are no silly or ridiculous answers.

It can take a little while to find your flow and to actually put the words on paper, especially if you haven't done anything like this before. Just be patient.

To start you off, here are some of the fears I've harbored and identified in my life:

- I am afraid that I will lose the online communities I have built

- I am afraid the content I create will be poorly received

- I'm afraid of being canceled

- I'm afraid of not having enough money

- I'm afraid of having to start again

- I'm afraid of bringing my past traumas into my present relationships

- I'm afraid of making mistakes

- I'm afraid of hurting people

- I'm afraid I'll quit if I don't reach my goals

- I'm afraid of quitting before I reach my goals

- I'm afraid I won't be able to provide for my family

These are just a few examples that came to my mind, but it's evident that the vast majority of my fears come from my past experiences. I have failed in the past. I have lived without money, I have struggled to support myself, and I'm afraid of history repeating itself.

Because I went through this process, I'm able to see that my fears could potentially be holding me back in so many areas of my life. If I'm scared of taking a risk, I won't take it, thus I'll never be able to progress in the things I want to do. I'll always be manifesting the reality that I'm scared of failing. And guess what, this means I'm going to manifest a failing reality, in this case one where I never even start what I set out to do.

By identifying your fears, you're able to recognize them when they pop up in your mind, and you'll notice when they're holding you back when you try to do something.

For example, if you want to progress in your career but you're afraid to ask for a promotion, you end up procrastinating and avoiding the promotion. You literally hold yourself back from being successful out of the fear of moving onto the next level.

In the workplace, you might come up with excuses for not chasing after the promotion, like saying you're too busy to handle more work, you haven't had the time to apply for a pending vacancy, or you might even sabotage how well you do a job. In reality, you may be afraid that you're not good enough for the role and you don't want to be rejected because it will crush your self-esteem.

This vibration of fear will then manifest in your reality and you'll never move forward. You'll be stuck in a fearful place as long as you have these thoughts.

Technique #5: Gaining Clarity with Intention

If you've ever read, watched, or listened to any kind of self-development content, you're definitely aware of the tip of writing down any of the goals you want to pursue. It's one of the most essential and necessary places to start on any self-development journey, Law of Attraction-based or otherwise. But why?

Well, the simple fact is that writing down your goals provides you with clarity about what you want. It helps you to be specific with your goals. The clearer you are, the more powerfully and accurately you'll be able to manifest the reality where those goals are fulfilled. Lack of clarity, or at least being unaware that you lack clarity, is an unconscious block in itself.

One of my favorite stories to quote is the story of Jim Carrey, Hollywood actor and comedian. In 1985, when Jim Carrey was starting out in Hollywood, he wrote himself a check dated Thanksgiving 1995. The amount on the check was $10 million. He folded it up and kept it in his wallet.

Turns out that in November 1995, Jim was cast for the second lead role in the hit movie franchise *Dumb and Dumber*, a contract that paid him $10 million. You could believe that this is a coincidence, but it's so concise in terms of date, time, and format that it's hard to pass off, especially when there are so many similar stories.

Carrey had taken the time to write a check, put the amount and the date on it, sign it, and carry it in his wallet. It's a very clear physical object that's incredibly specific, especially when you consider that you are paid using checks. The physical reminder of his manifestation was in his wallet for ten years, and it manifested.

But if you don't have a goal, or you're not clear on what you want, how can the universe help? It can't. You need to be as clear as possible with your desires if you want to manifest them.

Say you want money. Well, you could walk down the street and find a quarter and there you go. You have money. That's not a clear enough manifestation. You need to start asking yourself;

How much money do you want?

How do you want to receive it?

When do you want to receive it?

How long do you want it for?

What are you planning to do with it?

Are you worthy of having it?

Do you want it for the reasons that align with your values?

Are you willing to do what it takes to get it?

For this technique, say you want to manifest $500. Now ask these questions in order and see what answers you come up with. By going through this process, you'll be able to discover some of your unconscious blocks, which is the foundation to overcoming them.

Once you're able to overcome these obstacles, you'll be well on your way to manifesting the wealth, success, and abundance that you desire. Remember, it's not about having a certain dollar figure in your bank account, it's about having everything you need to live comfortably and achieve your goals without stress or worries related to money.

CHAPTER 4

The Secrets to Attracting Money

"Happiness is not in the mere possession of money; it lies in the joy of achievement, in the thrill of creative effort."
– Franklin D. Roosevelt

Several years ago, when I was trying to sort my life out, I was trying so hard to get some kind of foundation to pull myself out of my financial rut. It seemed like I was taking one step forward and two steps back. No matter how hard I was working and intentionally saving, I found myself back at square one so often it was completely demoralizing.

And it wasn't always outside my control. Every now and then I would have a bad week and end up making an impulsive purchase, or spending more than I wanted when I went out with friends for lunch. The shame and stress this made me feel was beyond words.

It took a long time, several months to a year in fact, to find some consistency, and it's only in hindsight that I finally figured out what was going on. I was spending all my time facing forward. I was setting up goals I wanted to hit, ways of life I wanted to manifest, and organizing the things I wanted to do, but it was my past and my unconscious beliefs that were holding me back.

It wasn't until I started following this process, through learning and mastering the Law of Attraction, that I started to make progress. Despite figuring out my past, beliefs, values, and unconscious blocks, I still wasn't there. Something was missing.

Yes, big steps were being made and I was doing so much better than I was in the past. Even going through the processes you've learned so far in this book will be enough to bring positive changes and manifestations to your life, but if you're really serious about going all the way and making long-term, sustainable differences that will change your life forever, you need to know how to use the Law of Attraction to actively manifest the life you want.

Imagine your life is a ship, sailing the oceans of existence. So far, we've gone around the ship and patched the holes and you're currently learning how to stay afloat. Now it's time to learn how to master the waves.

When it comes to attracting money, it's only once you've started o remove your unconscious blocks (which we covered in the previous chapters), that you'll create the space to focus on the positive manifestations of bringing wealth into your life. The processes of removing old blocks and replacing them with new ones go hand in hand.

Once you understand this, you can begin using the Law of Attraction to attract money into your life. Let's go right back to the basics with the aim of redefining how you look at money, unlocking the door for more accurate and powerful manifestations.

What is Money?

Money is an idea that has been created by humans to make trade easier. It is an agreement that certain items or services have a value and can be traded for other items or services. Money is not physical; it is an idea that exists in our minds.

Money is, therefore, a concept. Before money existed in the way we understand it today, objects of value were things like livestock, essential items, and even other human beings. It had to be a valuable item that could be easily traded.

Eventually, humans started using precious metals, such as gold and silver, to pay for goods. These metals were used because they were rare and had a lot of value. Today, most countries use paper money, which is backed by the government's promise to pay its value. In the United States, this paper money is called Federal Reserve notes.

Currently, money has evolved into a digital asset. It's seen as a figure on your mobile banking app or bank statement. It's seen in savings accounts or even in cryptocurrency wallets.

Now, why am I explaining this?

Well, when you're using the Law of Attraction, you need to be clear about what you're attracting. Without clarity and precision, you can manifest something you don't want. You have to be specific with your manifestations, which is why it pays to go through this process of seeking clarity regarding what you're after.

However, knowledge is not enough. Understanding is your foundation. You must take action.

Technique #6: Becoming Actionable and Proactive

You need to open your mind to the idea of taking action. Yes, the Law of Attraction is a powerful tool, but it will not, and cannot, manifest money into your life without your help.

You must take action and do whatever is necessary to bring money into your life. This may include setting goals and taking steps to achieve them, working hard, and being persistent. The Law of Attraction is way more than just a mindset.

The important thing to remember here is that to act is to show the universe you are really serious about what you're trying to manifest. This is a HUGE problem with a lot of self-help books and readers. So many people believe that simply reading self-development books will be enough to help them change, but that's not the case. Knowledge is knowledge. Action turns this knowledge into results.

If you have really big and ambitious goals, it can be overwhelming to think about what kind of steps you need to take that you end up taking none at all out of fear of not making the right choice or wasting your time.

There are going to be times you don't get things right and make mistakes, but that's okay. This is how you're going to learn the lessons you need to know to manifest more concisely.

Once you start taking action, you'll be able to figure out the details of your plan and overcome any obstacles that come your way.

Manifesting Money in Your Life

The first step is to get clear about what you want. Be specific and write down exactly how much money you want, in what form, and for what purpose.

We'll touch on this later when we dive into the strategies you can use when it comes to using the power of visualization to manifest wealth and success, but the clearer you can be with what you want, the more accurate your thoughts will be, and the more accurate your manifestations will be.

For example, let's say you're in debt and you want to move into a debt-free chapter of your life. You would need to take a proper look at your finances and figure out what you need. Let's explore this:

Debt = $5,000

Income = $1,000 per month

Outgoings (rent, bills, etc) = $900

When you're living off $100 per month, you're not going to be able to pay off your debt any time soon, so you need to think about ways to approach this in a way that works for you. For example, are you going to aim for a higher paid job, which means more income and more money to pay off your debt? Do you want to cut down on your spending and have more money to pay off the debt?

Get a clear plan.

The plan doesn't have to be perfect, but it has to be visualizable. So, if you want to get a better job, you can start visualizing yourself in a higher paid job. What would you be doing? What kind of paycheck would you be receiving? What would your office or building look like? What would your coworkers be like?

Again, we'll get into this more later on, but for now, the most important thing you can do is to go through the process of getting in touch with what you want and having a clear idea of the path you want to take.

Next, ensure that you're thinking about money in a positive way. As you're going through the process of defining what you want, take a moment to think about or at least write down some of the problems you think you might experience along the way. These are the unconscious blocks that are going to hold you back if you're not careful, which is why it's so important to become aware of them.

CHAPTER 5

The Money Trap and How to Get Out of It

As I was writing this book, I thought a lot about my past experiences and my journey with everything we've spoken about so far. I thought about the process, the wins, and challenges I faced on my path. However, there was one thought that kept coming up that I hadn't really addressed.

The thought that rich people aren't happy. There's quite a common idea that even if you have billions in the bank, you could be absolutely miserable, whereas if you have the bare minimum and no money, you can still live an incredibly happy life. Basically, money doesn't buy happiness, and this is something more and more people are sharing as the number of millionaires and billionaires rises around the world.

Why is it that people are not getting happier as they get richer and increase their financial wealth?

Well, quite simply, money and wealth are tangible. If you're a parent, it's very difficult to gauge whether you're a good parent. Because it's abstract, you're motivated just to do your best at the time, which is typically a really good approach because you learn and get better with time.

However, with money, you can see exactly how much money you have in the bank at any hour of the day. You can see when your money is up and when it's down, and if you invest in a portfolio, you'll have opportunities to see it go up and down second by second if you really wanted to. This means there's a ton of pressure to keep seeing yourself earn more, and this pressure can make you miserable.

That being said, the biggest cause of misery comes with the expectations you hold. The more you earn, the more you buy and the more you crave. The cost of your lifestyle increases; when someone living on $1,000 per month starts earning $10,000 per month, they still end up spending everything they earn because they are buying more.

Thus, there's a pressure to keep earning more so the craving can be satisfied, but because you're in this position where you're not manifesting more money, you're not happy, and you're not content with where you are. Your mind becomes obsessed with the chase. This is known as the 'money trap.'

The money trap is when you become so focused on making money and acquiring wealth that you forget about the things that are important to you. You may neglect your relationships, health, and happiness to focus on making more money.

Being in the money trap means you believe that having more money will solve all your problems and make you happy. However, this is not always the case.

In truth, if you're able to stay true to yourself and your values, you'll be far more satisfied with your journey because you're manifesting a life that's true to you rather than chasing material objects. Remember the concept of having a rich or poor mindset.

To get out of the money trap, you need to focus on the things that are important to you and remember why you want to make money. You should also set limits on how much money you will allow yourself to focus on at one time. This means that you should not let money become the only thing that matters to you.

However, this can feel a little abstract until you're able to adopt an actionable approach, so this is what we'll focus on now.

Escaping the Money Trap

When I started earning money and slowly began to make my way out of debt, I unconsciously made my way into the money trap. Having money was exciting. I suddenly had the opportunity to buy things that I never could afford before, and I wanted to treat myself.

It started with small things, like getting takeouts more often, or buying drinks for my friends at bars. It moved on to more expensive things, like signing a new, but rather expensive, phone contract for a nice new iPhone, and going out more to parties and nightclubs.

At the time, my long-term goals were to get a car, to work on my career, and to get an apartment so I could be independent and support myself, but lifestyle inflation (which we'll discuss in a minute), was keeping me in place. Despite earning more, I was still spending 95% of my income with no consideration for the future.

Because I wanted to sustain all the short-term, indulgent things,

I was sending out vibrations to the universe that these things were more important and valuable, thus this is what I attracted more of, and this was the reality I was manifesting.

When you focus on the things that are important to you and you remind yourself to stay focused on them, you'll be less likely to get trapped in the money trap. You will start to see money as a tool that can help you achieve your goals, rather than something that is more important than anything else.

Technique #7 - How to Avoid Lifestyle Inflation

Simply put, lifestyle inflation is where you spend more money as you earn more, so you actually stay exactly where you are in terms of wealth, especially over the long-term. This can take a lot of people by surprise, because even though they are earning more than they did a few years ago, they still have no savings, and if an unexpected bill appears, they struggle to pay it.

But how can this be the case if they're earning more?

Well, this is lifestyle inflation in full effect. Let's look at two people and their average spending.

Spending	Person #1	Person #2
Income	$1,000	$10,000
Rent	$600	$4,000
Clothes	$50	$500
Savings	$0	$100
Food and Bills	$350	$3000
Personal Luxuries	$50	$3000

As you can see, even though the prices on what person #1 and person #2 are spending is wildly different, they are both spending basically 100% of their income because they are prioritizing material goods. For example, Person #1 is struggling to afford anything, whereas Person #2 is earning more, but spending a large chunk of it on things like expensive car loans, vacations, fancy food, and so on.

If either person were to lose their jobs or their money, they would both be left with nothing and unable to sustain their current lifestyle. This way of living is unsustainable because it focuses on indulgence and greed, rather than wealth. Neither of these people have wealth, just lots of things.

In a sense, the two could be exactly the same person, just a few years apart and a few promotions or good work opportunities later. Because their attitude hasn't switched from a poor mindset to a rich one, lifestyle inflation keeps them where they are, and they will never be able to focus on long-term goals that provide them with value. They'll instead always be chasing more.

On the other hand, if we introduce Person #3 and Person #4, someone who starts in the same place as Person #1, but is able to adopt a rich mindset while avoiding lifestyle inflation, the tables will look a little different.

Spending	Person #3	Person #4
Income	$1,000	$10,000
Rent	$600	$1,500

Clothes	$50	$100
Savings	$0	$7000
Food and Bills	$350	$800
Personal Luxuries	$50	$800

Sure, these figures are just examples, but you can see that with $7,000 going into savings every month, this person has a large amount of wealth to fall back on. This means they are sustainably earning money so they are prepared for the future, and can focus more on what will bring value to their lives.

Remember, being rich refers to how much money you have, whereas being wealthy means how long you can have money for. Wealth is about having time to do the things you love. While having money is important, true wealth goes beyond that. It's about having a balance in all areas of your life – physical, mental, emotional, and spiritual. When you have this balance, you're able to focus on what's truly important and you become less attached to material things.

So, how do you do it?

1. Evaluate your spending habits.

First, be proactive in taking note of your current spending habits. Track your expenses for a month or two so that you have a clear idea where your money is going. This will help you identify any areas where you may be spending too much.

2. Create a budget.

Once you know where your money is going, it's time to create a budget. Determine how much you need to save and how much you can afford to spend each month. This will help keep you accountable and on track with your spending goals.

3. Make a plan.

Creating a budget is one thing, but actually following through with it is another. That's why it's important to have a plan – a specific roadmap outlining the steps you need to take to achieve your financial goals. If you need help creating a plan, there are many online resources available that you can look into.

4. Be mindful of your triggers.

We all have spending triggers – things that make us want to

spend money even when we don't necessarily need to. Maybe it's a new outfit that catches your eye, or an irresistible sale at your favorite store. The key is to be mindful of these triggers and avoid them as much as possible.

5. Find alternative ways to treat yourself.

It's important to have some fun in your life, but that doesn't mean you always have to spend money to do it. There are many fun and affordable activities you can enjoy without breaking the bank. For example, take a walk in the park, watch a movie at home, or have a picnic with friends.

6. Invest in yourself.

One of the best things you can do for your financial health is to invest in yourself. This means taking steps to improve your knowledge and understanding of financial matters. There are many great books and articles on personal finance available online and in libraries. Additionally, there are plenty of free or low-cost financial education courses offered online and by community organizations.

7. Seek professional help.

If you're having trouble getting out of the money trap on your own, seek professional help from a qualified financial advisor. They can assist you in creating a budget, finding ways to reduce your expenses, and reaching your financial goals.

By going through these actions, you're showing the universe that this is what you really want. You're showing that you want to be mindful of your spending and you don't want to fall into the money trap and you're not focused on just buying material goods, but instead being wealthy in all areas of your life, and using money as a tool to look after your family.

Even if you're sitting down to write your budget and you don't actually get around to working out 100% of the details, you're putting out the energy that you want this reality to take place. Even though you might not have every detail of your future or your plan figured out, it will come in time once this reality starts to manifest.

It takes time, action, and patience for everything to start falling into place, but if you can go through the process, it will happen. When you're able to adopt this way of living your life, you'll be able to get out of the trap and start making money in a more positive and meaningful way.

CHAPTER 6

The Language of Success

"When you change the language you use to talk about your goals, you change the odds of achieving them."
- Tony Robbins

How do you speak? What kind of words do you use? Of course, this isn't going to be a question you ask yourself very often. When you speak to someone and they respond, the chances are you just speak your mind and chat about whatever you want to talk about. You engage in conversation at a real-time pace, perhaps with slight pauses for processing what the other person said and conjuring a response.

When you're thinking, you're most likely thinking about the content of the thoughts, rather than the thoughts themselves, or more specifically, how those thoughts are worded.

With the Law of Attraction, the words you speak and the words your thoughts are made from are of utmost importance. You could follow every single technique in this book, but if you don't follow this one, it would all be for nothing because your language is dictating that you'll manifest a reality that doesn't align with the one you want.

Let's break this down.

The Importance of Language

One of the most powerful books I've ever read is *The Four Agreements* by Don Miguel Ruiz. Based on Toltec concepts, an ancient culture that dates back to pre-Columbian MesoAmerican times, Ruiz explains how words are magic and that there is so much power in the words you say to yourself, the words you think, and the words you give to others.

It's all about choice and power. While I highly recommend reading this wonderful book yourself, the four agreements you'll find inside the pages are as follows;

- Be impeccable with your word and never use it against yourself or others.

- You can't take things personally if you have a strong sense of self.

- Ask questions instead of making assumptions.

- Always do your best, even if your best changes.

While there's certainly wisdom in each of these agreements, our focus is on the first. So, what does it mean?

Well, words are magic. Words are power. How you speak to someone and the words you use can make or break someone depending on the content and the way they are spoken.

A simple 'You can do this' can raise someone out of such a dark place, whereas a 'Will you please be quiet?' could shatter someone's self-esteem and confidence for years. It may sound extreme, and that's because it is.

To explain this concept, Ruiz tells the story of a mother and a daughter having a conversation. The mother has had a very stressful day at work and is trying to relax at home. Her young daughter gets home from school and is singing in the most amazing, most angelic voice. However, the mother, who's stressed and isn't really acting mindfully, says something along the lines of 'Can you be quiet? You're giving me a headache.'

The way this is said can be crushing to a child, and usually is.

The daughter grows up believing that her singing gives other people headaches, and thus she doesn't sing, ultimately depriving the world of her beautiful voice, and preventing her from doing something she loves and enjoys.

Such is the power of words. Flippant use of words can cause long-term damage, and while this example is about two people, the same logic applies to how you speak to yourself.

How often do you catch yourself saying something along the lines of;

- I'm so stupid for saying and doing that

- I can't do this, I'm not good enough

- I look so fat today

- I'm far too shy/scared to do something like that

- I would never be able to stand up like you did

Every time you say something along these lines, you are making an agreement with yourself. You are affirming how you feel about something because you're stating it as a fact, and your brain doesn't know the difference between a flippant thought and a fact. It's just taking in all that information and processing it.

According to the Law of Attraction, like attracts like, and so the language/magic/agreement you put out into the universe is the language you get back.

Substituting Your Language

In order to manifest your desires, you need to be clear and specific about what you want. This means using words that are aligned with your goal, and speaking them out loud or writing them down. You're also going to make sure your language is positive, showcasing that you're confident and fully believe in what you're saying.

Think about how you might look at yourself in the mirror from time to time and think 'Oh, I'm putting on so much weight. I feel really unconfident.' Notice how you say it with certainty. You see it and you 100% believe it is a fact, but now imagine saying instead, 'I am a magnet for wealth and success.'

Are you able to say such statements with the same deliberate certainty? If you're not, then this isn't the reality you'll manifest. If you're able to say 'I am a magnet for wealth and success,' today and believe in yourself, but next week you say something like 'I am so bad at managing my money and everything I try to do to save doesn't work,' then your conflicting statements will cancel out.

In this situation, you'll remain stuck in the same place without making any progress. If you're using more negative language than positive language, you'll move backwards and find yourself experiencing more and more problems.

So, it's important that you get into the habit of using affirmative statements such as 'I am confident,' 'I am healthy and full of vitality,' or 'I attract wealth and abundance into my life.' The more you use these kinds of phrases, the more familiar they will become to you and the more natural it will feel to say them. As you become more comfortable with using these phrases, you'll find that your beliefs will start to change and you'll start to see evidence of the Law of Attraction working in your life.

Negative self-talk is a very common obstacle that prevents people from achieving their goals and manifesting their desires. If you find yourself stuck in a cycle of negative thinking, it's time to make a conscious effort to change your language and start speaking words of positivity and power. Remember, your thoughts become your reality, so choose them wisely!

A really easy way to remember this is to avoid using negative-oriented language like 'can't,' 'won't,' and 'don't,' when talking about your goals. When you use this kind of language, you are telling the universe that you do not believe in yourself and that you are not confident.

The Power of Affirmations

We've all witnessed situations where someone is about to do something scary. It could be speaking in front of a large crowd, bungee jumping, asking someone out on a date, attempting to perform a trick or a stunt, or going to a job interview. What do people instinctively do in these situations to hype themselves up?

They recite affirmations. They talk to themselves. They may mutter something under their breath, like 'I can do this,' or 'You've got this, this is what you've trained for!' These are affirmations that people are using to put themselves in the mindset of achieving whatever they want to achieve.

After all, if you aren't telling yourself that you're going to do something, you're not going to do it. The opposite is also true.

In my own life, I used affirmations daily to put myself into the state of mind where I'm focused on what I want to do and what I want to achieve. Thus, I'm sending out controlled energy into the universe about what I want to achieve. For example, if I want to write five pages of this book today, I say something like;

"I am creative and let the words flow naturally from my mind"

"I am focused and purposeful when it comes to fulfilling my goals"

"I have all the energy I need to create and work hard"

By thinking and saying them out loud, and, most powerfully, writing them down, I'm sending an instruction to the universe of what I want to achieve. And, because the universe is always listening, it will do its best to give me what I've asked for.

It's not just about thinking or saying these affirmations, you have to truly believe them. If you don't believe that you can achieve what you're setting out to do, the universe will sense that lack of belief and it won't work. The more conviction and belief you put into your affirmations, the better they will work.

So, how can you use affirmations in your life to get what you want? It's actually pretty simple.

Deep Diving into Affirmations

Affirmations are statements you recite to yourself on a daily basis. They are meant to help you change the way you think about yourself and your goals. When you recite affirmations, you are telling yourself that you can achieve your goals and that you are confident in yourself.

Affirmations can be helpful in achieving your goals because they help to change the way you think about yourself. When you start to believe in yourself and your abilities, you are more likely to achieve your goals.

Affirmations can also help you attract positive energy and achieve your goals faster. When you are focused on your goals and have positive energy surrounding you, you are more likely to achieve them.

In order to use affirmations to achieve your goals, you need to recite them on a daily basis. This means that you should say them in the morning and evening, and whenever you feel like you need a boost of confidence.

Technique #8: Using Affirmations to Manifest Your Desires

The first step is to figure out what you want. What is your goal? What is your desire? Be as specific as possible.

Next, write down your affirmations. Make sure they are in the present tense, and they are positive statements. For example, don't write 'I will not fail.' Instead, write 'I am confident and successful.'

Now, the key is to repeat these affirmations to yourself as often as possible. Remember, the more repetitive you are and the more conviction you have, the more energy you're putting out into the universe, and the more seriously you'll attract what you want.

You can say them out loud, you can mutter them under your breath, or you can write them in a notebook to read over and over again.

Another great way to use affirmations is to record yourself saying them, and then play the recording back to yourself as often as possible. This is especially effective if you have difficulty believing the affirmations yourself.

When you do this, really put feeling and emotion into your voice. The more feeling you can put into it, the better. This will help your subconscious mind take in the affirmations and start to believe them.

A fantastic way to remember how important repetition is comes from my old martial arts teacher. There's a well-known theory from Malcolm Gladwell, a journalist and writer, who popularized the '10,000-hour rule,' which suggests that you need to practice something for 10,000 hours to become a master at it, whatever it is that you want to do.

However, this concept has been around for a long time. When you picture ancient monks in the mountains of Nepal, all standing in a line in meditative poses, or sitting still for hours every single day, they are putting in those hours to achieve a certain outcome.

My martial arts teacher had a similar idea where he'd say you need to practice something ten times to understand it, 100 times to learn it, 1,000 times to be good at it, and 10,000 times to master it.

The same concept applies to affirmations. Say something ten times, you grasp it, but if you're saying it 10,000 times, there's no doubt it's going to become your truth. And it works both ways. If you're looking at your reflection and telling yourself that you don't like what you see potentially hundreds of times a day, this is what you're affirming, and the reality you're manifesting.

Instead, take control of your thoughts, notice when you're affirming negative statements and work on letting them go. Be proactive in practicing and exclaiming your positive affirmations.

Research suggests that we have an average of 6,000 thoughts a day, so it's important to realize just how much of an impact these thoughts are having in your life and where they're taking you.

Technique #9: How to Create Powerful Positive Affirmations

It's important to make sure you're using clear and concise language when it comes to manifesting. So, how can you do this to create the affirmations you want to work with?

It's actually pretty simple. You need to make sure that you're using affirmative statements that are in the present tense. For example, don't say 'I will be rich.' Instead, say 'I am rich.'

Make sure that your affirmations are something you can believe. If you don't believe them, your subconscious mind won't either, and it won't work. So make sure that they are realistic for you.

Finally, keep your affirmations short and concise. The shorter they are, the easier they are to remember, and the more conviction you can put into them when you're repeating them.

Some examples of powerful affirmations you can use are:

- I am healthy and happy.

- I love my life and I am grateful for all that I have.

- I am surrounded by positive, like-minded people.

- I attract abundance and success into my life.

- I am deserving of love, happiness, and all good things.

These are just a few examples, but you can use any affirmation that resonates with you and you can believe in. The most important thing is that you're putting time and effort into repeating them regularly.

It's always important to figure out what works for you. My definition of wealth could be different from yours, which is why you need to take time to clearly describe what you want and what the language means to you and your perceptions.

Technique #10: How to Replace Negative Thoughts with Positive Ones

While you want to work proactively on bringing positive affirmations into your life and making them a daily part of your life (more on this in the next section), you need to work on identifying and phasing out the negative affirmations that are going through your mind.

These negative affirmations could be anything, for example;

- I'm not good enough.

- I'll never achieve my dreams.

- I don't deserve happiness.

- I'm not lovable.

and so on.

The problem is that these could be thoughts you've been

affirming for years, to the point that they're just habitual and you're not even aware of them.

But that doesn't mean they're not impacting your life in a negative way. If anything, it's likely they have an even bigger impact since you're so used to them and they've become a big part of your belief system.

To identify these negative affirmations, start by taking some time to introspect and reflect. Check in with yourself regularly throughout the day and listen to your internal dialogue. When you catch yourself thinking something negative, take a step back and try to identify where this thought is coming from.

Is it something that's based in reality or is it just a general feeling? Once you've identified the source of these negative thoughts, work on releasing them. A lot of the time, these thoughts are based on fears or past experiences that are no longer relevant, so it's important to let them go.

A great process to adopt is to write them down on a piece of paper and then rip it up or burn it as a physical way of releasing them. You can also work on reframing these negative thoughts into positive ones. For example, if you catch yourself thinking 'I'm not good enough,' try replacing it with 'I am deserving of love and happiness.'

It might take some time to get used to this new way of thinking, but eventually, these positive affirmations will become second nature to you. It does take time and a ton of awareness because you're literally rewiring your brain, but if you're working on this process daily, then you're setting yourself up for success.

Technique #11: How to Develop a Daily Affirmations Practice

Okay, so now that you know what affirmations are and how to identify the positive and negative ones in your life, it's time to start working on developing a regular affirmations practice.

You'll need to be intentional about this practice because results will not be seen overnight. You're essentially trying to create a new habit, which takes time, effort, and consistency.

Here are a few tips to help you get started:

1. Choose affirmations that resonate with you

It's important that you choose affirmations that really resonate with you. If they don't resonate with you, it's going to be a lot harder to make them a part of your daily life.

To find affirmations that resonate with you, start by brainstorming a list of things you want to work on or manifest in your life. Once you have this list, look for affirmations that align with these goals.

For example, if you want to manifest more abundance in your life, you might choose affirmations like 'I am worthy of abundance,' or 'I am open to receiving all the good that life has to offer.'

2. Make them a part of your daily routine

One of the best ways to make something a habit is to integrate it into your existing daily routine. This makes it a lot easier because you're not trying to force something new into your life, you're just slotting it into a time that's already dedicated to something else.

For example, if you always brush your teeth first thing in the morning, you can add in a quick affirmation session at that time as well. Putting a Post-It note on your mirror that you read every morning can be a great way to have a little reminder to help you adopt this process.

Just take a minute or two to say your affirmations out loud (or in your head if you're not comfortable doing it out loud) and really focus on believing them.

3. Repeat, repeat, repeat

Repetition is key when it comes to making affirmations a part of your life. The more you say them, the easier they are to believe. So, don't be afraid to really go overboard with repeating them throughout the day.

You can say them whenever you have a free moment, such as when you're in the shower, cooking dinner, or taking a break at work. You can even set a reminder on your phone a few times throughout the day so that you don't forget.

4. Be patient

Developing a regular affirmations practice is creating a new habit. And, as we all know, forming new habits takes time. So, be patient with yourself and do not get discouraged if you don't see results immediately.

Just keep at it and eventually, it will become second nature. Trust me, the effort is worth it!

5. Be consistent

The final (and arguably most important) tip is to be consistent with your affirmations practice. This means making a commitment to do it every day, no matter what.

Of course, there will be days when you'll be too busy, too tired, or you'll miss a day. That's totally okay. Just pick up where you left off and don't beat yourself up over it. The fact that you're going through the process is another way of communicating to the universe that you're serious, creating the reality you crave.

Make regular effort to make affirmations a part of your life. If you can do that, then you're well on your way to manifesting all your deepest desires.

Technique #12: How to Use Affirmations to Attract Wealth

Of course, to tie this all in with the main theme of this book, I want to take a moment to explore how you can use affirmations to attract wealth.

While you can use affirmations for just about anything, they're particularly powerful when it comes to manifesting money. This is because our beliefs regarding money are often ingrained in us from a young age, and through the power of affirmations, as well as defining the language you use when thinking and talking about money, you can change things considerably.

For example, if you grew up hearing your parents say things like 'money doesn't grow on trees,' or 'we can't afford that,' it's likely that you've internalized those beliefs and they're impacting the way you think about, and handle money as an adult.

While we all know that money doesn't actually grow on trees, it's still a limiting belief because you're believing that money is limited when it's not. Money is everywhere. You just need to be open enough to receive it and let it come to you.

A very common example of this is when people have negative beliefs towards bills. It may sound strange, and it certainly took me a while to get my head around this one, but paying off a bill, especially a bill for credit or a loan you've taken out, can feel demoralizing. However, this is a primary example of a poor mindset.

Instead, paying money for a service you use is actually a sign that you're capable and financially sound. The credit provider trusted that you were capable of managing the loan and making the proper repayments, and this is a sign that you can handle your finances and are responsible. This is the kind of mindset you need your affirmations to have.

After all, if you have negative beliefs about money, it's going to be very difficult to manifest more of it into your life. If you're putting out negative energy when it comes to money, that's what you're going to get back.

By using positive affirmations, you can start to shift your beliefs and put yourself on the path to attracting more wealth.

To help you get started, here are a few of my favorite wealth affirmations:

- I am worthy of abundance.

- I am open to receiving all the good that life has to offer.

- I am responsible with money.

- I am grateful for all the money I have in my life.

- I can build a solid financial foundation for myself.

- My finances are improving.

- I am allowed to have money.

- I make intelligent decisions with my money.

- I spend responsibly, and am happy about that.

- I am able to control any spending impulses I may have.

- I enjoy managing my money properly.

- I am comfortable when I manage my money well.

- I am worthy of having money.

- Money comes to me easily.

- Money is drawn to me effortlessly.

- I trust myself enough to make beneficial financial decisions.

- Income comes to me through multiple channels.

- Wealth is a solid and reliable part of my life experience.

- I attract wealth and success easily and effortlessly.

- My life is rich and fulfilling.

- I deserve to be prosperous and successful.

This is a nice big list of affirmations that you can use as a foundation for your own. Feel free to use these ones, or create your own, depending on what your focus is and what's important to you. The trick, as with every aspect of the Law of Attraction, is to be as concise as possible.

It really helps to take a moment to reflect on your life to see what really matters to you, to see what you're struggling with, and then create affirmations that reflect your goals and desires. For example, if you're struggling to pay off debt, use affirmations to not only ensure you're in control of your debt and are making responsible financial decisions, but also to express mental clarity that you have money coming your way.

It's important to really feel the emotions behind the affirmations as you say them. So, take a moment to close your eyes and picture yourself having already achieved your goal of attracting more wealth into your life. Really feel what that would be like and let those positive emotions guide you as you speak the affirmations.

From here, the technique is simple. Simply write down three to five affirmations you want to focus on and repeat them twice a day, for three to five minutes. You can do this while self-meditating, or by using a guided meditation that reflects your affirmations. You can say them in your head, but it's better if you say them out loud or write them down over and over again.

You'll see the changes happen fast, because you're literally rewiring your brain to think in a different way, sending out different, conscious energy to the universe, which is the energy you'll get back. When you're faced with choices, your mind will be in the right place to make the best decision that serves you. You can always stick with the same affirmations, or you can mix them up after a week to reflect what you're now focused on.

If you practice affirmations regularly, you'll start to see a shift in your beliefs and your relationship with money. And, as your beliefs change, you'll start to see more evidence of wealth in your life.

So, don't underestimate the power of using affirmations to attract wealth into your life!

CHAPTER 7

Eliminating Limiting Beliefs

We've covered a ton of information and techniques pertaining to the Law of Attraction, but it's worth mentioning one of the consistent problems that will keep coming up in your practice. It doesn't matter how much work you're putting into your positive affirmations and actions, if you have limiting beliefs that you don't address and work to heal and overcome, you'll remain stuck.

Limiting beliefs is one of the biggest roadblocks to achieving your goals. They hold you back from achieving your goals, and include thoughts like 'I'm not good enough,' or 'I can't do this.'

Limiting beliefs can sabotage your success and keep you from achieving your goals. In order to achieve your goals, you need to get rid of any limiting beliefs that are holding you back. Let's explore this.

What are Limiting Beliefs?

A belief is just a thought that you keep thinking. A limiting belief is a negative thought that's holding you back from achieving your goals.

For example, let's say that your goal is to get a new job, but you believe that you're not good enough or qualified enough to get it. So, even though you may be perfectly qualified for the position and you've done everything right, your limiting beliefs will prevent you from submitting your application.

Your mind is a very powerful tool, and what you believe ultimately becomes your reality.

One of the best examples of a limiting belief comes from the adage of an elephant at the circus. When the circus gets the elephant as a baby, they tie it up to a stake where it can't move. No matter how hard the elephant tries to pull at the stake, it's tied up.

As time passes, the elephant gives up and no longer tries to escape because it believes it's tied up. However, as the elephant gets older and bigger, there's no doubt in anyone's mind that the elephant has the strength and muscle needed to pull up the tiny stake that was once able to hold it in place.

However, due to the hard-wired belief that the stake holds it in place, a belief that was developed for years, the elephant won't even attempt to escape. Yet, all the elephant would have to do is to try and pull the stake out of the ground, and it would be free.

In your own life, you may have a belief that's holding you back, but that doesn't mean it's true. Just because you believe something doesn't make it true.

How do Limiting Beliefs Form?

Most of our limiting beliefs are formed in childhood. They're usually the result of something that happened to us that we interpreted in a negative way.

For example, let's say that you were constantly told that you were stupid. As a result, you grow up believing that you are stupid and that you could never achieve anything in life.

These types of experiences can have a profound effect on our lives and can shape our beliefs about ourselves.

Other times, our limiting beliefs are the result of outside influences such as the media or what we see on social media. We may see someone who's successful and think to ourselves, 'I could never be like that,' or 'I could never have what they have.'

These outside influences can also shape our beliefs about ourselves and our abilities.

No matter how your limiting beliefs were formed, they're holding you back from achieving your goals, and it's important to get rid of them.

Technique #13: Identifying Your Limiting Beliefs

The first step to overcoming your limiting beliefs is identifying them. You might not even be aware of the fact that you have them. Once you're able to identify your limiting beliefs, you can start to work on changing them.

There are a few ways to identify your limiting beliefs:

- Pay attention to your self-talk: The things you say to yourself on a regular basis provide a big clue as to what your limiting beliefs are. If you find yourself regularly saying things like 'I can't do this,' or 'I'm not good enough,' those are likely some of your limiting beliefs.

- Pay attention to your emotions: Your emotions can also clue you in to what your limiting beliefs might be. If you find yourself feeling scared or anxious about something, that's a sign that there might be a limiting belief lurking underneath.

- Pay attention to your results: Another way to identify your limiting beliefs is to look at your results. If you're not getting the results you want in life, it's a good indication that something may be holding you back.

Once you've identified some of your limiting beliefs, it's time to start working on changing them.

Technique #14: How to Change Your Limiting Beliefs

Once you're aware of the beliefs that are holding you back, you can start to work on changing them.

There are a few ways to change your limiting beliefs:

- **Use positive affirmations**: Positive affirmations are a great way to start changing your limiting beliefs. By repeating positive statements about yourself and your abilities, you can start to reprogram your mind and change the way you think about yourself.

- **Visualize yourself achieving your goals**: Another way to change your limiting beliefs is to visualize yourself achieving your goals. When you see yourself succeeding, it's easier to believe that you can actually achieve your goals. This helps to override any negative self-talk or doubts that might be holding you back.

- **Take action towards your goals**: Finally, taking action towards your goals is a great way to change your limiting beliefs. When you take action and start making progress, it's easier to believe that you can actually achieve your goals. This helps to boost your confidence and eliminate any doubts that might be holding you back.

Eliminating limiting beliefs is an important step in achieving your goals. When you get rid of the beliefs that are holding you back, you open yourself up to new possibilities. You can achieve anything you set your mind to when you believe in yourself and focus on your goals.

Limiting Beliefs Surrounding Wealth and Success

There are a lot of limiting beliefs surrounding wealth and success. People often think that to become wealthy, they will have to give up their time with family and friends, or that they will no longer be able to enjoy life. This is simply not true!

You can be happy without being wealthy or successful. While it's important to focus on what you want in life, do not let your current circumstances define your happiness.

So, what are your limiting beliefs surrounding wealth? What are your limiting beliefs surrounding success? Are you willing to work hard to overcome them?

A common limiting belief is that you'll have to give up all your free time if you want to be successful or wealthy. After all, how else are you going to find the hours to build everything you want to build, whether it's starting a business or saving money? This is a common belief instilled by society.

The truth is, you don't have to give up your free time to be wealthy or successful. In fact, sacrificing your free time can actually lead to more problems down the road. When you don't have any hobbies or activities outside of work, you can start to feel burned out and resentful. This can lead to job dissatisfaction, which will impact your wealth and success in the long run.

It's important to remember that wealth and success are not synonymous with each other. You can be wealthy without being successful, and vice versa. While it's great to have both, it's not necessary for happiness. So, if you're currently feeling stuck in a rut, don't be afraid to take some time for yourself and focus on your happiness. After all, that's the most important thing in life!

Now, the tricky bit is understanding and identifying what your own limiting beliefs towards wealth and success are. This can be difficult because a lot of the time they are subconscious. Once you become aware of them, however, you can start to work on overcoming them.

Some common limiting beliefs pertaining to wealth and success include;

- I'll never be good enough for wealth and success

- I don't have the drive, determination, or work ethic other people have

- I don't deserve it

- It's not possible for me

- I'm not ready yet

- I don't have the skills or knowledge to do what I want to do

- I don't know what steps to take next

- There's too many people already doing what I want to do

- People in my life will think I'm stupid for trying

- I will be judged by society

- If I fail, everyone will laugh at me

All these beliefs stem from a lack of self-confidence or self-belief. If you don't believe in yourself, it will be difficult to achieve anything in life. This is why it's so important to work on your mindset and belief system around wealth and success.

When it comes to this process, take time to figure out what your limiting beliefs are and work out where they came from. How did you adopt them? Was it through family? Society? The culture you grew up in? Something you saw online, in a book, or on television? Once you know where they came from, it will be easier to start to work on changing them.

Remember, you can achieve anything you want in life if you're willing to put in the work. So, don't let your limiting beliefs hold you back any longer! Start working on overcoming them today. The quicker you get started, the quicker the changes will happen and the easier it will be. The longer you wait, the more ingrained your current thinking will become, and the harder it will be to break free.

If you're not sure where to start, a great place is with positive affirmations.

Positive affirmations are statements that you repeat to yourself on a daily basis in order to change your mindset and beliefs. For example, some wealth and success-related affirmations could be;

- I am worthy of wealth and success

- I am capable of achieving anything I set my mind to

- I deserve to be happy and prosperous

- I am willing to put in the work required to achieve my goals

- I am open to new opportunities and possibilities

- I am grateful for all the abundance in my life

These affirmations will help to change your mindset around wealth and success, and eventually, your limiting beliefs will start to shift as well. In some cases, it can happen almost instantly, and you'll be amazed with how following through with these for a few days can make such a big difference, but more on this later.

Give it a try and see how you feel! Remember, it takes time to change your mindset, so be patient with yourself and keep at it. Wealth and success are attainable for anyone who believes in themselves.

CHAPTER 8

A Deep Dive on Gratitude

Any experienced Law of Attraction practitioner knows that there's one vital practice that will guarantee your success; not only when it comes to manifesting, but also when it comes to living a happy, prosperous, and fulfilling life. And it is even more important when we're working on bringing wealth and success into your life.

I am, of course, talking about gratitude.

Gratitude is the language of the Universe. It is the one thing that always brings us more of what we want, whether it be love, money, success, or anything else.

But we often get caught up in our own heads, worrying about what we don't have and all the things we think are wrong with our lives. This kind of negative thinking only serves to keep us stuck and attracting more of the same into our lives.

To utilize the Law of Attraction to its full potential, it is essential to change your language from negative to positive. This means making a conscious effort to focus on all the good in your life, no matter how small it may seem. Every time you catch yourself thinking or speaking negatively about something, stop and consciously change it to a positive.

For example, if you're worried about not having enough money, instead of thinking 'I can't afford that,' tell yourself 'I'm attracting more wealth into my life every day.' If you're unhappy with your job, instead of thinking 'this job sucks,' tell yourself 'I'm grateful for this job because it is helping me get closer to my dream career.'

It may seem like a small change, but over time it will make a big difference in the way you think, feel, and attract things into your life. So, make a commitment to yourself to start speaking the language of gratitude and watch as your life starts to change for the better.

There's also a hard truth you need to learn now.

If you're not happy, content, and grateful with your life now, you're not going to be happy in the future, even if you manifest wealth and success. This is because telling yourself 'I'll be happy when I reach this goal, and only when I reach this goal,' you're basically giving yourself permission to be unhappy until that goal is reached.

It's much better to focus on being happy now and let the Universe take care of the rest. That doesn't mean you can't aim big and try to bring wealth and success into your life. That doesn't mean you can't grow and have goals that you want to fulfill. These will certainly help you live a complete and satisfying life. The problem is that if you develop an ungrateful and always-striving-for-something mindset, even if you reach those goals, you'll never be happy and satisfied. You'll just be aiming for the next thing, thinking that you'll be happy and fulfilled when you get there.

The Importance of Gratitude

Gratitude is a funny thing. We often think that we'll be grateful for something when we get it, but the truth is, gratitude is a state of mind. It's an attitude that we choose to adopt, regardless of our circumstances.

This means that we can be grateful even when things are tough.

In fact, this is when gratitude is most important.

When we're going through a difficult time, it can be easy to focus on all the negative things that are happening and forget about the good. But if we can find even one thing to be grateful for, it can completely change our perspective.

Take, for example, someone who has lost their job. It would be easy for them to focus on all the negative aspects of their situation: they're worried about how they're going to pay the bills, they're stressed about finding another job, they're feeling down about themselves.

But if that person can find even one thing to be grateful for, maybe they have a supportive partner, or they're healthy, or they have a roof over their head, then that can help them to see the situation in a more positive light.

And when we see things in a more positive light, we're more likely to take action and do something about our situation. We're more likely to believe that things will work out for us and be open to new opportunities.

So if you want to start using the Law of Attraction to its full potential, make a commitment to be grateful for everything, no matter how small it may seem. Of course, this is all easy in theory, but when times are tough and you're feeling the weight of life pushing down on your shoulders, it's easy to get lost in the thoughts and reactive emotions that come up. This is why it's important to embrace a daily gratitude practice to build up your gratitude mindset.

Technique #15: Starting Your Own Gratitude Practice

The best way to develop an attitude of gratitude is to start your own gratitude practice. This can be something as simple as taking a few minutes each day to sit down and think about or write down the things you're grateful for.

You might want to do this first thing in the morning, so you can set the tone for the day ahead, or last thing at night, so you can reflect on the good things that have happened during the day.

Or you might want to do it at random times throughout the day. The important thing is that you make it a regular habit so that it becomes second nature.

There are many different ways to go about this, but here are a few suggestions:

- Keep a gratitude journal and write down three things you're grateful for each day.

- Say out loud, "I'm grateful for _____" whenever you remember throughout the day.

- Think of one thing you're grateful for each time you brush your teeth.

- Before you go to bed, think of three things that have happened during the day that made you smile or feel good.

The key is finding a method that works for you and stick with it. The more regularly you practice, the easier it will be to develop an attitude of gratitude.

But what if I don't have anything to be grateful for?

If you're thinking, 'I don't have anything to be grateful for,' then you're not looking hard enough. There's always something to be grateful for, no matter how small it is.

It could be the fact that you woke up this morning, you have a roof over your head, or you had a good cup of coffee. It doesn't matter how big or small it is, there's always something.

And if you're really struggling to find something, think about the things that you take for granted. These are the things that we often don't realize are important until they're gone.

For example, we might not think about how lucky we are to have running water and a flush toilet until our city is hit by a natural disaster and we're left without these things.

Or we might not realize how lucky we are to have our health until we fall ill.

These are the things that we should be grateful for because they're so easy to take for granted.

So next time you find yourself thinking, 'I don't have anything to be grateful for,' just remember that there's always something. The more you practice gratitude, the easier it will be to find things to appreciate in your life.

Using Gratitude to Create Abundance

One of the best ways to use gratitude is to create abundance in your life. When you're grateful for what you have, you open yourself up to receiving more.

It's like saying to the Universe, 'I'm grateful for what I have, and

I'm ready to receive more.'

The Law of Attraction is all about energy. What you put out there is what you get back. So if you want to attract more abundance into your life, start by being grateful for the abundance that you already have.

This doesn't mean that you have to be grateful for everything in your life. It's perfectly normal to have negative feelings like anger, sadness, and frustration.

But it's important to focus on the positive as much as you can, so that you can attract more of what you want into your life.

Here are a few ways to use gratitude to create abundance in your life:

- Start each day by thinking of three things you're grateful for. This sets the tone for the rest of the day and helps you to focus on the positive.

- Before you go to bed, think of three things that happened during the day that made you feel good. This helps you to end the day on a positive note and go to sleep with good energy.

- Whenever you get a chance during the day, take a moment

to appreciate the little things. For example, if you're out for a walk, take a moment to appreciate the fresh air, the sunshine, and the beauty of nature around you.

- Whenever you receive something, take a moment to appreciate it. Whether it's a gift, a raise at work, or just a compliment from a friend, take a moment to really appreciate it and feel grateful for it.

The more you focus on gratitude, the more abundance you will attract into your life. So start using gratitude today to create the life of your dreams. Cultivating gratitude can positively affect so many areas of your life, so it's highly recommended you take time trying to figure out what kind of gratitude practice works for you. Here are a few tips to remember.

The most basic practice is to keep a gratitude journal, or to start journaling, or keeping a diary and taking a few minutes to write about the things you're grateful about. This is an approach recommended by Berkeley University. Your process can be as simple or as progressive as you like. You may just bullet point a few things a day, or go into detail about what you're grateful for and why. It's important to remember that it doesn't matter how big, small, significant, or vague these things are. The fact is you're paying attention to what you can be grateful for.

- **Keep a Journal**

Create a daily practice of writing down what you're grateful for. Talk about things you enjoy. Try to braindump your thoughts without thinking too much about it or judging your thoughts. Just express whatever comes to mind since this is where you'll find true clarity in what you believe and how your mind works. From being grateful to the people you love or the color of the sky, to having a roof over your head or even that your favorite food exists. It can even be past experiences or memories.

- **Don't Discount the Bad**

It's important to remember that you can't just be grateful for the good things that have happened in your life, but also for the bad experiences. The bad experiences we go through help to shape us and make us who we are today, and who we will be in the future, and if you're aiming to be the best version of yourself, then these experiences are essential.

Remember how far you've come, what you've made possible, and all the hardships you've conquered and survived. Appreciating the good and the bad is a great way to cultivate gratitude.

- **Use Your Senses**

There are going to be days when it's hard to be grateful. This might be because of the mood you're in, or it may be hard to focus. In times like this, it can be incredibly powerful to tune into your senses.

Take a moment to tune in to all five senses; touch, sight, smell, taste, and hearing. Be grateful to the sensations that these senses give you. Once you start treating and looking at the human body as a gift, gratitude can amplify dramatically.

If you want to take a really specific approach to cultivating gratitude in certain areas of your life, such as the areas we're covering in this book, maybe even an area you feel like you're stuck in, then you can take a more actionable approach to gratitude.

Choose a topic, like money, relationships, career, family, or health, and focus on only giving thanks in that area for 30 days - use your journal or at least write down 3-5 affirmations. After 30 days, you'll notice a huge difference in this area of your life and your perspective on it.

- **Have the Hard Conversations**

You don't have to be best friends with everyone you know, but it is important to work on your relationships and to be grateful for the people in your life. Be sure that while you might not like someone, you still respect them and appreciate who they are.

If there are issues or problems within a relationship, then it's important to address these issues head-on. This will help keep the problem from getting out of hand and will make both parties feel more secure in the relationship.

And yes, this can be challenging, but it is worth it when you want to cultivate gratitude in your relationships, especially if one or both people aren't aware that their actions are affecting the other person negatively.

- **Show Gratitude to People Around You**

One of the best ways to show people that you're grateful for them is to actually tell them. This can be done in person, or even over the phone or through text. It is important to take action and not just think about being grateful.

A great way to do this is to write a letter expressing your gratitude. You can even do this anonymously if you want. This is a really beautiful way to show someone how much they mean to you and how much you appreciate them without making it awkward.

This applies to literally anyone, whether it's the people within your inner circles, or people within your community, like a shopkeeper, a bus driver, or someone on the other end of a customer service line. Be genuinely grateful to people, express it. The energy you'll be putting out in the universe is an energy like none you've ever experienced before.

- **Do Something Nice for Someone**

Another amazing way to show people that you care and that you're grateful for them is by doing something nice for them, whether it's big or small. In the age of social media, we're often bombarded by images of acts of kindness and seemingly random people going out of their way for someone. However, even a small act can have a huge impact on the recipient.

A great way to do this is to pay for someone's coffee behind you in line at Starbucks, buy someone's groceries at the grocery store without them knowing it's you who paid for them, or sending flowers anonymously to your loved one just as a surprise.

Practicing gratitude every day will transform your life dramatically. Whether you're struggling with something specific or not, cultivating gratitude and practicing it consistently can only benefit you. So set aside time each day and try some or all of these methods - your life will thank you for it!

And, don't forget that the language you use is important. The universe is always listening, and if you're constantly putting out negative energy, that's what you're going to get back. Be mindful of your words and try to focus on the positive as much as you can.

CHAPTER 9

The Law of Abundance

Throughout this book, we've covered a lot of topics, with the focus on wealth and success in general, but what about abundance? Well, while it certainly ties into everything we've discussed already, the Law of Attraction is connected to another law; the Law of Abundance.

The Law of Abundance is a universal law that governs the flow of energy in the universe. The Law of Abundance states that there is enough for everyone, and that you can attract wealth and abundance into your life by opening yourself up to receive it.

When you apply the Law of Abundance, you are aligning yourself with the flow of energy in the universe. You are opening yourself up to receive all the good things that are available to you.

When you apply the Law of Abundance, you are not asking for more than you need. You are simply asking for what is already available to you. This law ensures that there is enough for everyone. When you open yourself up to receive, you allow it to work in your favor.

What is Abundance?

Abundance is the state of having more than enough. It is the state of being prosperous or successful. When you are in a state of abundance, you have everything you need and more. However, this extends to more than just yourself.

There's a common limiting belief that you can't have something or you can't succeed in your pursuits because there are already so many people doing what you want to do, so how could there possibly be room in the world for you as well?

For example, how could you possibly be a famous and successful movie star when there are already so many? It's so competitive, so do you really have a chance?

Go into any bookshop and you'll see hundreds of thousands of books written by authors that span centuries, many award-winning and known by millions, and those who have never sold a copy. How would you possibly be able to shine in a world like this?

The fact is, there's room for everyone. When you understand and apply the Law of Abundance, you realize that there's more than enough for everyone to have what they want in life.

Wealth, success, love - these things are not finite. They are not limited. There is no competition when it comes to attracting these things into your life.

The Law of Abundance states that there is enough for everyone. It doesn't matter how many people are already doing what you want to do or how competitive it may seem. You can still have everything you want in life.

There are, however, a lot of factors that play into this. If you're thinking that you're not going to be able to bring success and wealth into your life because too many other people have got what you want and you wouldn't be able to get there, then you're sending out the energy to the universe that you're not worthy or capable, thus it becomes a limiting belief.

Take what you want to do in life. Do you want to be an actor like Will Smith? Do you want to sell as many books as J. K. Rowling? Do you want a nice secure house and loving family like your neighbor? Do you want to earn $150,000 a year like your boss?

Why can't you? What's stopping you? Why can't you write and sell as many books as J. K. Rowling? Because she's already doing it? You don't have a good enough idea? You're not a good enough writer?

All of these are just excuses. The truth is, there is nothing stopping you from achieving any level of success that you want in life. You can have anything you want. It's just a matter of opening yourself up to receive it.

Technique #16: How to Open Up to the Law of Abundance

The first step to opening up to the Law of Abundance is to become aware of your own thoughts and emotions about money. Do you have any negative beliefs about money? Do you think that money is evil or that it's the root of all evil?

If so, these are limiting beliefs that you need to get rid of.

Another way to open yourself up to the Law of Abundance is to start thinking and talking about money in a positive way. Instead of saying things like, 'I can't afford that,' start saying things like, 'I am attracting abundance into my life.'

When you start thinking and talking about money in a positive way, you will start to see results. The more you focus on the good things that money can do for you, the more good things will come into your life.

The third way to open yourself up to the Law of Abundance is to take action towards your goals. If you want to attract wealth and abundance into your life, start taking steps to achieve your goals. The more action you take, the closer you will get to achieving your goals and the more likely you are to attract wealth and abundance into your life.

The more you apply these concepts and techniques, the more you will open yourself up to the Law of Abundance. When you start living in abundance, you will see that there is more than enough for everyone to have what they want in life. You will also start attracting all the good things that you desire into your life.

CHAPTER 10

The Power of Visualization

In these final chapters, our main focus has been on the powerful techniques you can use to really bring your manifestations to life, and visualization is one of the best. There's no way you're going to manifest the reality you want to the degree you want it without developing a consistent visualization process or technique.

An Introduction to Visualization

First, let's do a quick refresher on what visualization is. Visualization is the practice of seeing things in your mind's eye as if they're already happening in your life. This could be anything from imagining yourself driving your dream car to picture yourself on stage accepting an award.

When you can see it happening in your mind, you're much more likely to make it happen in real life because you'll be vibrating at the frequency of your desire and attracting it into your life.

For example, if you want to manifest a new job, it's not enough to just see yourself in the role. You also have to imagine how it feels to get the offer, start your first day, and receive your first paycheck. The more real you can make it feel in your mind, the better chance you have of making it happen in real life.

Arnold Schwarzenegger is a fantastic example of putting this into practice. During his younger years, he would take part in bodybuilding competitions all over the US, and he would reportedly spend time walking around the events while visualizing what it would be like to win the competition. He would even go so far as to imagine what it would feel like to have the trophy in his hands, hearing the crowd cheering his name, shaking hands with the other competitors, and seeing his name in the paper.

Of course, we all know that Arnold Schwarzenegger went on to become one of the most successful bodybuilders of all time, winning Mr. Olympia seven times, more than anyone else in history, and he regularly talks about how he attributes a lot of his success to visualization.

You have everything you could ever need to tap into this superpower. You just need to know what you're doing and how to use it properly.

The Benefits of Visualization

Humans are visual creatures. We are constantly bombarded with visual information, and we process this information in ways that other animals cannot. This is why visualization is such a powerful tool. When you visualize something, you're able to see it in a completely different way than if you were just looking at it with your eyes.

Visualization can help us see things in a new light, and it can also help us attract what we want in life. The Law of Attraction states that like attracts like. So, if we focus on positive thoughts and images, we will attract positive experiences into our lives. Likewise, if we focus on negative thoughts and images, we will attract negative experiences.

Visualization is a great way to focus on positive thoughts and images, and it can be used to attract anything you desire. You can use visualization to attract success, love, money, or anything else you can imagine. The sky's the limit!

When you visualize something, you are essentially creating a blueprint for what you want to manifest in your life. The more specific and detailed you can be, the better. The better you can see it, the more likely it is to happen.

When you visualize something, you're going through the process in your mind of what you're going to do and how you're going to do it, as well as making it real.

Just like Arnold Schwarzenegger acted like the winner in his contests before he was the winner, he sent out the energy to the universe that he wanted to win and what it would be like. Joe Templin, the author of *Everyday Excellence*, ultramarathon runner, and guest on the We're All Humans Here podcast, talks about how he used visualization to help him win a martial arts tournament.

He visualized exactly how he was going to win in incredible detail: What his foot felt like flying through the air, the position and angles of his body, the feeling of his clothes, the atmosphere of the room, and how the collision itself felt when in action.

On the day, Templin won with the same knock-out kick he visualized. For the crowd, it was the first time they'd seen him win. For him, it was well over the 100,000th time he completed the kick, combining both the practice kicks in the dojo and the countless kicks he visualized in his mind.

How Does Visualization Work?

The power of visualization is based on the Law of Attraction. The Law of Attraction states that you attract what you focus on. When you visualize what you want, you are focusing on your goals and putting yourself in a position to achieve them.

When you visualize, you are sending a message and all the necessary vibrations to the universe that you want what you are seeing. The universe responds to this message by giving you more of what you want. When you focus on your goals, you are telling the universe that you are ready to receive them.

The universe will then start to give you opportunities to achieve your goals.

Technique #17: How to Visualize and Manifest Your Dreams

As with every other technique in this book, you first need to be absolutely clear about what you're trying to manifest. The more clarity you have, the better your visualization will be.

Take time to think of and identify your goals. Write them down in any way that makes them tangible to you. What is it that you want to achieve? What are your dreams and aspirations? Once you have a good understanding of what you want, you can start to visualize it.

See yourself achieving your goal in your mind's eye. Make it as real as possible. Feel the emotions you would feel if you were already living your dream life.

For example, if you want to manifest a new car, see yourself driving it. Feel the wind in your hair and the sun on your skin. Smell the new car smell. What does it feel like to turn the wheels in your hand? How does it feel to see it on your driveway? How does it feel to drive around with your family, music playing, and a beautiful destination on the way?

The more real you can make it feel in your mind, the better chance you have of making it happen in real life because you'll be vibrating at the frequency of your desire and attracting it into your life.

It's important to spend time each day visualizing what you want to achieve. You can do this first thing in the morning or last thing at night. It doesn't matter when you do it, as long as you do it regularly.

Remember, the more time you spend visualizing your goals, the more likely you are to achieve them because you'll be putting all of your focus and energy on what you want to achieve.

Time for a little practice.

Visualization is such a powerful process and while it's ideal for manifesting large dreams and fulfilling your goals, you can also see its power on a small scale. This is one of the best ways to witness the power of the process. When you're convinced, you'll then be able to apply it successfully to much bigger and more significant manifestations.

So, think about what you're doing today or tomorrow and highlight something that is important to you. Maybe you're at work or you're spending time with your partner or crush.

Take ten minutes to visualize how you want these interactions to go. See yourself in the situation and really feel how you want to feel.

If it's work, see yourself being productive and feeling good about what you're doing. If it's your partner or crush, imagine spending time together and enjoying each other's company. See yourselves laughing and having fun.

Feel the positive emotions associated with these situations and let them flow through you. Feel the happiness, love, and contentment. Feel what it feels like to work hard at your computer. Feel the keys under your fingers and the feelings of sending emails or securing a contract with a new client.

Feel what it's like to cuddle and hold your partner. Think about what you're doing, whether you're playing a game, watching a movie, or going for a walk. What does the environment feel like? What are you talking about? What tone of voice are you and your partner using? What does it feel like to hold their hand?

This is the kind of detail you want to implement. The more real you can make it feel in your mind, the better. This is all about putting yourself in a positive mindset and feeling good about what's to come.

When you've spent some time visualizing what you want to achieve, really let it sink in and believe that it will happen. Trust that the Universe will provide for you.

Now, live your life knowing that you've already set the scene for success by taking the time to visualize how you want things to go. You may be surprised at just how well things start to go for you when you do this regularly!

The power of visualization is one of the most important tools you can use to manifest your dreams. When you visualize what you want, you are putting yourself in a position to achieve it. Use affirmative statements and include as many senses as possible to make your visualization as realistic as possible. Practice regularly and be patient – your dreams will eventually become a reality.

CHAPTER 11

Letting Go of Perfectionism

And with all this under our belt and fresh in your mind, we have come to the last chapter. When I set out to write this book, I never thought this would be something I would include. I didn't really give it much thought until I realized how powerful it is when it comes to working towards goals, manifesting wealth and success, and not standing in your own way.

Perfectionism is a powerful obstacle and one of the biggest stumbling blocks you'll encounter on your journey. For example, writing this book, I had an idea in my head of how I wanted it to be, but if I were to rigidly stick with this idea and not allow for the creative process to take over, I would suffer the constraint of perfectionism, and the book would never be completed or released.

It's essential to realize that as you head towards the manifested life you want to live, there are going to be things that happen that you don't want. There are going to be situations that hurt and are difficult to deal with.

For example, let's say you're trying to do something creative. It could be you're trying to write a book, write a song, learn an instrument, or create a website or logo for your new business idea. It can be any part of your life.

You spend hours on your project, research how to do it, practice creative affirmations, and put in the work, but you can't seem to get it right. You're stuck and you can't find your way forward. You start to get disheartened that you're not getting anywhere, and doubt creeps in. Your language has changed, which means your energy has changed, and your pursuit is hitting a deadend because that's the reality you're manifesting. This is how your perfectionism is holding you back.

The truth is, there's no such thing as perfect. Not only will the traits of perfectionism increase how self-critical you are and ultimately lower your self-esteem to the point where you'll give up and fail, but you'll become unsatisfied and unfulfilled with your life. You won't get anywhere because you're only focused on the result, rather than the journey, and the fact you never finish anything will continue to hit hard.

So, how do you get over this?

First, the techniques you've learned will help. Through these practices, you'll come to learn that the journey is the satisfying part of life and that the end goal is only part of it. Say you're writing a book, you'll have much more fun developing the characters than you will selling copies. However, when you're learning to sell copies and market your book, that's a whole new process to enjoy.

You're going to come across obstacles on every single journey no matter what you choose to spend your time on, but as long as you can remember that they are a part of the journey, you'll get through it.

The trick to real manifestation comes from being able to trust the process. You may have a general idea in your head of what you want, probably a pretty clear idea of what you want if you're visualizing it properly, but you need to be flexible.

What you think you want may not come to you in the way you want it, and you need to go through the stranger, previously unforeseeable events, to get there. If you're not flexible, you'll never allow the process to unfold as it should and you may find yourself getting in your own way.

It's also important to remember that when it comes down to it, you're not going to be able to change or control everything in your life, but what you can change is your attitude and how you react to the things that happen. If you can maintain a positive outlook, stay focused on what you want, and be open-minded and flexible with the process, you'll find that working towards manifesting your dream life will be far easier than if you were stuck in perfectionism.

Addressing Perfectionism

Perfectionism is the need to have everything perfect. However, when you are a perfectionist, you often set unreasonably high standards for yourself. You find it difficult to accept criticism, and you are never happy with your work.

This causes so many problems, like anxiety, depression, and low self-esteem.

When you are a perfectionist, it is extremely difficult to take risks. You are so afraid of making mistakes that you often don't try new things. This limits your opportunities for growth and development.

For example, if you are a perfectionist, you might be afraid to start your own business because you are afraid of failing. You might not apply for that dream job because you think you're not good enough.

Perfectionism also stands in the way of progress. If you're a perfectionist, it's very difficult to finish anything. You often get bogged down in the details and can't see the forest from the trees. This means that projects often take much longer than they need to, and they are often never completed.

This is a problem because it means that you never get to experience the satisfaction of completing something. It also means that you miss out on opportunities to learn from your mistakes.

So how do you overcome perfectionism?

If you want to use the Law of Attraction to its full potential, you need to work on addressing your perfectionism. You need to learn to accept yourself for who you are and be okay with making mistakes.

You also need to learn to take risks. This doesn't mean that you should recklessly jump into things without thinking first. But it does mean that you should be willing to try new things and put yourself out there.

And finally, you need to learn to let go of the need for everything to be perfect. You need to be able to finish things and be okay with them not being perfect.

This might sound like a lot of work, but it's worth it if you want to use the Law of Attraction to manifest your dream life. Remember, the more flexible you are, the easier it will be to trust the process and let go of perfectionism.

It's important to remember that when it comes down to it, you're not going to be able to change or control everything in your life, but what you can change is your attitude and how you react to the things that happen. If you're able to keep a positive outlook, stay focused on what you want, and be open-minded and flexible with the process, you'll find that working towards manifesting your dream life will be far easier than if you were stuck in perfectionism.

One of the most important things to remember when using the Law of Attraction is that your attitude and how you react to the things that happen in your life are just as important as what you do. You need to stay focused on what you want, keep a positive outlook, and be willing to take risks and make mistakes. If you can do this, then you'll find that working towards your dream life will be far easier than if you were stuck in perfectionism.

Of course, it's always nice to have an actionable approach to these things, so here are some tips to remember and try to implement throughout your life.

- **Set realistic standards for yourself**

You can do this by taking a look at your past successes and failures and setting standards based on those. From here, you can start to slowly raise your standards as you become more comfortable with taking risks.

- **Start small**

If you're working on a project, start with something that you know you can complete and then build from there. This will help to increase your confidence and show you that you're capable of completing things, even if they're not perfect.

- **Focus on the process, not the outcome**

This is especially important when it comes to manifesting your dream life. It's easy to get caught up in wanting everything to be perfect, but it's important to remember that the journey is just as important as the destination. Enjoy the process and trust that everything will work out in the end.

- **Be willing to make mistakes**

Remember that you're human and that making mistakes is part of the process. Don't beat yourself up over them and learn from them so that you can avoid making the same mistakes in the future.

- **Have faith in the process**

The Law of Attraction is a powerful tool, but it's only going to work if you believe in it. Have faith that things will work out and trust that the universe has your back.

Unlike the other techniques we've explored throughout this book, this is not really something you can practice as a daily practice. It is to be applied in the moment. However, if you can keep these tips in mind and try to implement them into your life, you'll find that using the Law of Attraction will be far easier than if you were stuck in perfectionism. Try to let go of any perfectionist tendencies you have and focus on what you want. Remember, the more flexible you are, the easier it will be to trust the process and let go of perfectionism.

Then the more you start to see the results for yourself, the more you'll believe in the power of the Law of Attraction!

Conclusion

And with that, we come to the end of this book, and the start of the next chapter of your journey. Throughout this book, we've covered what you need to know when it comes to using the Law of Attraction to manifest and attract wealth, success, and abundance in your life.

I hope that you've enjoyed reading it as much as I've enjoyed writing it, and most importantly, I hope that you feel armed with the knowledge and tools you need to change your life for the better using the universal power that is the Law of Attraction.

Remember, the Law of Attraction is always working in your life whether you realize it or not. The better aligned you are with your desired outcomes, the more easily they will come to fruition. So keep visualizing, stay positive, take inspired action steps, and watch as your life transforms before your very eyes!

For now, that's all from me. I will continue using these techniques in my own life, on my goals and dreams, and continue to manifest more books and a life I'm happy to wake up to. To help with this journey, I would love to hear your feedback.

Wherever you picked up a copy of this book, leave a review letting me know your thoughts and feelings on using the Law of Attraction.

You can also contact me on social media, as I am always happy to hear from my readers! Thank you so much for being here, and I hope this book has helped you as much as it has helped me.

Good luck on your manifestation journey, and I'll see you in the next book!

Thank You

"Happiness springs from doing good and helping
others."
— Plato

Those who help others without any expectations in return
experience more fulfillment, have higher levels of success, and
live longer.

I want to create the opportunity for you to do this during this
reading experience. For this, I have a very simple question... If
it didn't cost you money, would you help someone you've never
met before, even if you never got credit for it? If so, I want to
ask for a favor on behalf of someone you do not know and likely
never will. They are just like you and me, or perhaps how you
were a few years ago...Less experienced, filled with the desire
to help the world, seeking good information but not sure where

to look…this is where you can help. The only way for us at Dreamlifepress to accomplish our mission of helping people on their spiritual growth journey is to first, reach them. And most people do judge a book by its reviews. So, if you have found this book helpful, would you please take a quick moment right now to leave an honest review of the book? It will cost you nothing and less than 60 seconds. Your review will help a stranger find this book and benefit from it.

One more person finds peace and happiness…one more person may find their passion in life…one more person experience a transformation that otherwise would never have happened…To make that come true, all you have to do is to leave a review. If you're on audible, click on the three dots in the top right of your screen, rate and review. If you're reading on a e-reader or kindle, just scroll to the bottom of the book, then swipe up and it will ask for a review. If this doesn't work, you can go to the book page on amazon or wherever store you purchased this from and leave a review from that page.

PS - If you feel good about helping an unknown person, you are my kind of people. I'm excited to continue helping you in your spiritual growth journey.

PPS - A little life hack - if you introduce something valuable to someone, they naturally associate that value to you. If you think this book can benefit anyone you know, send this book their way and build goodwill. From the bottom of my heart, thank you.

Your biggest fan – **Layla**

www.ingramcontent.com/pod-product-compliance
Lightning Source LLC
Chambersburg PA
CBHW051001140626
46546CB00017B/2152